Pra
The Legacy of Pope John Paul II

This book is a treasury for research, reflection, and meditation. Keep it available, read it, and use it regularly.

Father Michael Scanlan, TOR
President Emeritus, Franciscan University of Steubenville

Not many people have the time or background to read and understand all of John Paul II's encyclicals. Alan Schreck has done us all a great service in clearly and carefully bringing out the essential points of all the encyclicals.

Ralph Martin
Sacred Heart Major Seminary, Detroit, Michigan

What the popes have taught over the past fifty years provides the correct way to interpret what the Church has announced since the Second Vatican Council. The bulk of post-conciliar papal instruction comes from the pen of Blessed Pope John Paul II. The present volume should encourage its readers to study carefully the 14 encyclicals that Dr. Schreck epitomizes.

Father Romanus Cessario, OP
Saint John's Seminary, Brighton, Massachusetts

As one who prepares people to be catechists and religious educators, I really appreciate this recent work of Alan Schreck. Here again in *The Legacy of Pope John Paul II,* he breaks down more scholarly writing into accessible language. The reflection questions and suggestions for further reading at the end of each chapter help facilitate a systematic study of the central teachings of this brilliant but pastoral pope, who conveyed the truth in love.

Sr. M. Johanna Paruch, FGSM, Ph.D
Professor of Catechetics, Franciscan University of Steubenville

The
Legacy of
—— Pope John Paul II ——

CATECHETICAL INSTITUTE
FRANCISCAN UNIVERSITY

Also in collaboration with Emmaus Road Publishing:

The Pedagogy of God
Caroline Fahey • *Waltraud Linnig* • *Sr. M. Johanna Paruch, FSGM*

The
Legacy of
—— Pope John Paul II ——

The Central Teaching of His 14 Encyclical Letters

——— Alan Schreck ———

EMMAUS
ROAD
PUBLISHING

Steubenville, Ohio
A Division of Catholics United for the Faith
www.emmausroad.org

EMMAUS
ROAD
PUBLISHING

Emmaus Road Publishing
827 North Fourth Street
Steubenville, Ohio 43952

Library of Congress Control Number: 2012937393
ISBN: 978-1-937155-36-0

Cover design and layout by Julie Davis, General Glyphics, Inc., Dallas, Texas (www.glyphnet.com)

Cover artwork: Tereza M Hazelton, "Pope John Paul II writing a letter" oil on canvas/ used with permission Tereza's Art Gallery http://tsartgallery.com

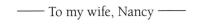 To my wife, Nancy ──

Contents

Abbreviations

CHURCH DOCUMENTS

AI   Paul VI, *Anno Ineunte*, Apostolic Brief to the Patriarch Athenagoras I (July 25, 1967)

CA   John Paul II, *Centesimus Annus*, Encyclical on the Centenary of *Rerum Novarum* (May 1, 1991)

Catechism   The Holy See, *Catechism of the Catholic Church*, Definitive Edition (1997)

CIC   The Holy See, *Code of Canon Law (1983)*

Compendium The Holy See, *Compendium—Catechism of the Catholic Church* (2005)

CT   John Paul II, *Catechesi Tradendae*, Apostolic Exhortation on Catechesis in Our Time (October 16, 1979)

DM   John Paul II, *Dives in Misericordia*, Encyclical on the Mercy of God (November 30, 1980)

DV   Second Vatican Council, *Dei Verbum*, Dogmatic Constitution on Divine Revelation (November 18, 1965)

DetV   John Paul II, *Dominum et Vivificantem*, Encyclical on the Holy Spirit in the Life of the Church and the World (May 18, 1986)

DVit   Sacred Congregation for the Doctrine of the Faith, *Donum Vitae*, Instruction on Respect for Human Life (February 22, 1987)

EE   John Paul II, *Ecclesia de Eucharistia*, Encyclical on the Eucharist in its Relationship to the Church (April 17, 2003)

EN   Paul VI, *Evangelii Nuntiandi*, Apostolic Exhortation on Evangelization in the Modern World (December 8, 1975)

EV   John Paul II, *Evangelium Vitae*, Encyclical on the Value and Inviolability of Human Life (March 25, 1995)

FR	John Paul II, *Fides et Ratio*, Encyclical on the Relationship between Faith and Reason (September 14, 1998)
GS	Second Vatican Council, *Gaudium et Spes*, Pastoral Constitution on the Church in the Modern World (December 7, 1965)
IB	Sacred Congregation for the Doctrine of the Faith, *Iura et Bona*, Declaration on Euthanasia (May 5, 1980)
LE	John Paul II, *Laborem Exercens*, Encyclical on Human Work on the ninetieth anniversary of *Rerum Novarum* (September 14, 1981)
LG	Second Vatican Council, *Lumen Gentium*, Dogmatic Constitution on the Church (November 21, 1964)
MF	Paul VI, *Mysterium Fidei*, Encyclical on the Holy Eucharist (September 3, 1965)
NCCB	National Conference of Catholic Bishops
NMI	John Paul II, *Novo Millennio Ineunte*, Apostolic Letter at the Close of the Great Jubilee of the Year 2000 (January 6, 2001)
PO	Second Vatican Council, *Presbyterorum Ordinis*, Decree on the Ministry and Life of Priests (December 7, 1965)
PP	Paul VI, *Populorum Progressio*, Encyclical on the Development of Peoples (March 26, 1967)
RH	John Paul II, *Redemptor Hominis*, Encyclical on Redemption and the Dignity of the Human Race (March 4, 1979)
RMat	John Paul II, *Redemptoris Mater*, Encyclical on the Blessed Virgin Mary in the Life of the Pilgrim Church (March 25, 1987)
RMiss	John Paul II, *Redemptoris Missio*, Encyclical on the Permanent Validity of the Church's Missionary Mandate (December 7, 1990)
RN	Leo XIII, *Rerum Novarum*, Encyclical on Capital and Labour (May 15, 1891)
SA	John Paul II, *Slavorum Apostoli*, Encyclical on the Eleventh Centenary of the Evangelizing Work of Saints Cyril and Methodius (June 2, 1985)
SRS	John Paul II, *Sollicitudo Rei Socialis*, Encyclical for the twentieth anniversary of *Populorum Progressio* (December 30, 1987)

UR	Second Vatican Council, *Unitatis Redintegratio*, Decree on Ecumenism (November 21, 1964)
UUS	John Paul II, *Ut Unum Sint*, Encyclical on Commitment to Ecumenism (May 25, 1995)
USCCB	United States Conference of Catholic Bishops
VS	John Paul II, *Veritatis Splendor*, Encyclical regarding Certain Fundamental Questions of the Church's Moral Teaching (August 6, 1993)

THE OLD TESTAMENT

Gen.	Genesis	Song	Song of Solomon
Ex.	Exodus	Wis.	Wisdom
Lev.	Leviticus	Sir.	Sirach (Ecclesiasticus)
Num.	Numbers	Is.	Isaiah
Deut.	Deuteronomy	Jer.	Jeremiah
Josh.	Joshua	Lam.	Lamentations
Judg.	Judges	Bar.	Baruch
Ruth	Ruth	Ezek.	Ezekiel
1 Sam.	1 Samuel	Dan.	Daniel
2 Sam.	2 Samuel	Hos.	Hosea
1 Kings	1 Kings	Joel	Joel
2 Kings	2 Kings	Amos	Amos
1 Chron.	1 Chronicles	Obad.	Obadiah
2 Chron.	2 Chronicles	Jon.	Jonah
Ezra	Ezra	Mic.	Micah
Neh.	Nehemiah	Nahum	Nahum
Tob.	Tobit	Hab.	Habakkuk
Jud.	Judith	Zeph.	Zephaniah
Esther	Esther	Hag.	Haggai
Job	Job	Zech.	Zechariah
Ps.	Psalms	Mal.	Malachi
Prov.	Proverbs	1 Mac.	1 Maccabees
Eccles.	Ecclesiastes	2 Mac.	2 Maccabees

THE NEW TESTAMENT

Mt.	Matthew	1 Tim.	1 Timothy
Mk.	Mark	2 Tim.	2 Timothy
Lk.	Luke	Tit.	Titus
Jn.	John	Philem.	Philemon
Acts	Acts of the Apostles	Heb.	Hebrews
Rom.	Romans	Jas.	James
1 Cor.	1 Corinthians	1 Pet.	1 Peter
2 Cor.	2 Corinthians	2 Pet.	2 Peter
Gal.	Galatians	1 Jn.	1 John
Eph.	Ephesians	2 Jn.	2 John
Phil.	Philippians	3 Jn.	3 John
Col.	Colossians	Jude	Jude
1 Thess.	1 Thessalonians	Rev.	Revelation
2 Thess.	2 Thessalonians		(Apocalypse)

Editor's Note

While *The Legacy of Pope John Paul II* may be appreciated by a wide audience of people who loved our late Holy Father—at the time of this first printing *Blessed* John Paul II—we have included extra material at the end of each chapter to help facilitate personal and group reflection on the important teachings presented in his encyclical letters. These may be used in adult faith formation classes or for the ongoing formation of catechists so that they may better understand the teachings of the Church. Also, by having all the encyclical letters collected in one book, we hope the readers may not only come away with greater insight into each teaching, but also see them as a unified body of truths, each one hinging upon the other.

For the fullest benefit from these reflections, after reading Dr. Schreck's summary and commentary on each encyclical, consider reading the entire encyclical on your own. All the papal documents are made freely available online at www.vatican.va (as well as the *Catechism of the Catholic Church*), or in book format through Catholic bookstores. And for the really dedicated "student," there are suggestions for further reading. Additionally, while the encyclicals are listed in chronological order, it is advisable to group them thematically when you study them (e.g., those covering social issues, or those relating to the Trinity). What may raise questions in one topical letter may be answered in another.

Lastly, a word of thanks to Dr. Petroc Willey, Editor of *The Sower* catechetical journal in Birmingham, UK, who first published Dr. Schreck's initial articles on these encyclicals in a series called, "The Heritage of John Paul II." Now everyone may reap the fruits of *The Sower*. May the Lord of the harvest rain down his grace to quench our souls and make us fertile soil, where his Word can take root and bear good fruit that lasts . . . as he did with Pope John Paul II.

Introduction

In the two-thousand-year history of the papacy, proclaiming and teaching the Gospel of Jesus Christ has always been central to the popes' mission and ministry. As St. Peter concluded the Church's first sermon on the day of Pentecost: "Let all the house of Israel therefore know assuredly that God has made him both Lord and Christ, this Jesus whom you crucified" (Acts 2:36).

This proclamation echoes through centuries at the heart of Christian and papal teaching. Popes are also the Church's chief shepherds; and while the responsibilities of governing the Church and addressing challenges from the world preoccupied many popes, others recognized their primary responsibility to proclaim and teach the Gospel. In recent times, I observe almost a new kind of papacy that emphasizes leading the Church through teaching, exemplified by popes such as Leo XIII (pope 1878–1903). I would go so far as to characterize the popes of the nineteenth and twentieth centuries (and now into the twenty-first century) as "teaching popes." While they certainly carry out their priestly and pastoral duties faithfully, they lead the Church mainly by their example and teaching. Since the Second Vatican Council, the "style" of that teaching has changed somewhat, moving away from a *Magisterium* concerned primarily with warnings and condemnations of false teachings to a teaching style that seeks to instruct positively about the Catholic faith and the positive implications and applications of the Gospel in today's world. Pope John XXIII recommended and followed this approach, as he expressed it his opening speech to the bishops at the Second Vatican Council, a council that he initiated. He declared:

> The Catholic Church, raising the torch of religious truth by means of this Ecumenical Council, desires to show herself to be the loving mother of all, benign, patient, full of mercy and goodness toward the brethren who are separated from her. To mankind,

oppressed by so many difficulties, the Church says, as Peter said to the poor who begged alms from him: "I have neither gold nor silver, but what I have I give you; in the name of Jesus Christ of Nazareth, rise and walk" (Acts 3:6). In other words, the Church does not offer to the men of today riches that pass, nor does she promise them a merely earthly happiness. But she distributes to them the goods of divine grace which, raising men to the dignity of sons of God, are the most efficacious safeguards and aid toward a more human life. She opens the fountain of her life-giving doctrine which allows men, enlightened by the light of Christ, to understand well what they really are, what their lofty dignity and their purpose are, and finally through her children, she spreads everywhere the fullness of Christian charity, than which nothing is more effective in eradicating the seeds of discord, nothing more efficacious in promoting concord, just peace, and the brotherly unity of all. (Oct. 11, 1962, no. 7)

I believe that what Pope John XXIII stated about the teaching of the Second Vatican Council also characterizes the teaching of Pope John Paul II. This should not surprise us, as young Bishop Karol Wojtyla was decisively formed and shaped by his experience at the Council, as he himself stated in his book, *Sources of Renewal: The Implementation of Vatican II*, first published in Polish in 1972, then in English in 1979.

IMPORTANCE OF ENCYCLICAL LETTERS

John Paul II was a "teaching pope"—a pope who led the Church and influenced the world primarily by the example of his life (his holiness) and by his teaching. In modern times, the encyclical letter has been the instrument for popes to express their most important teaching. While an encyclical letter may be presented to commemorate a particular event or feast day, its importance and application transcends that event or occasion. This teaching has lasting importance and value for the Church, and often for the whole world.

This is the importance of becoming familiar with the encyclical letters of Pope John Paul II. His encyclicals are what he believed to be most important for him to teach as pope to the Church and to the world. Therefore, it is no coincidence that his first encyclical letter is a proclamation of Jesus Christ, as was St. Peter's first message on the day of Pentecost. Then within his first five encyclical letters he completes his Trinitarian teaching with letters on the mercy of the Father (*Dives in Misericordia*) and on the Holy Spirit (*Dominum et Vivificantem*). As one of the bishops who worked to compose Vatican II's "Pastoral Constitution on the Church in the Modern World" (*Gaudium et Spes*), it was fitting as pope that he should continue to teach about important social issues, such as on human work (*Laborem Exercens*) and on the sanctity and protection of human life (*Evangelium Vitae*). It may seem odd to some that he should write an encyclical letter on the two saints Cyril and Methodius (*Slavorum Apostoli*), but not so odd once they recall that this was a Slavic pope who saw these two Slavic saints as bridges between Eastern and Western Christianity, not to mention between Eastern and Western Europe. Christian unity, a great concern of John Paul II's pontificate, is also the theme of his twelfth encyclical letter, *Ut Unum Sint*.

Knowing how devoted Pope John Paul II was to Mary, Mother of God, so much so as to make his papal motto Mary's own *Totus Tuus* (meaning "totally yours"), it is easy to understand that his writing of an encyclical on Mary (*Redemptoris Mater*), was simply a natural outpouring of his filial love for his Mother and Mother of the Church. He also set to pen and paper his passion for the evangelizing mission of the Church in the hope that all could be revitalized in faith and renew the Church. However, recognizing the damage of nihilistic philosophies and of relativistic cultural trends upon society, this profound Catholic philosopher set out to reaffirm "the splendor of the truth" and "the unity of faith and reason" in two separate encyclicals. Finally, his last and crowning encyclical letter (*Ecclesia de Eucharistia*) delves into the unsurpassable gift and mystery of the Eucharist, reflecting on the very heart of the mystery of Christ and of his Church.

Pope John Paul II left the Church with a legacy that will not be forgotten. It is a privilege to introduce you to this legacy by presenting some of the central themes and insights of John Paul II in his fourteen encyclical letters.

1

Redemptor Hominis
"The Redeemer of Man"

The First Encyclical Letter of Pope John Paul II

March 4, 1979

"The Redeemer of Man, Jesus Christ, is the center of the universe and of history." With these words, Pope John Paul II launched a pontificate focused on teaching the faith of the Church clearly and comprehensively. The mission of Pope John Paul II from the beginning has been to teach the rich tradition of the Catholic Church, especially as it is expressed in the Second Vatican Council, which he calls "the great grace bestowed on the Church in the twentieth century" (*NMI* 57).

STARTING FROM CHRIST

Pope John Paul began his pontificate speaking of the center of our faith: Jesus Christ. "Through the Incarnation," Pope John Paul says, "God gave human life the dimension that he intended [humanity] to have from his first beginning." The redemption won by Jesus Christ has set the human race free from "the original sin and the whole history of the sins of humanity." Truly, the Holy Father says, we are living in "a season of a new Advent, a season of expectation," especially as we look forward to the year 2000, "the year of a great Jubilee" which he says, we are "already approaching" (1.2).

KEY THEMES OF THE PONTIFICATE

It is remarkable to me that in the first article of his first encyclical letter in 1979, Pope John Paul II introduces the key themes of his pontificate. First, the Pope alludes to the beginnings of God's plan for the human race, which he discussed in great depth almost immediately in his Wednesday audiences. This teaching has been called his "theology of the body"—one dimension or aspect of Pope John Paul's "theology of the human person," which focuses on the dignity of the person originally made in God's image and likeness, then restored to that fullness through Jesus Christ.

Secondly, the Pope speaks about the significance of Jesus Christ in the present moment of history and sees the time of his pontificate as a "new Advent" preparing in anticipation of the celebration of Christianity's two thousandth anniversary—the "great Jubilee" of the year 2000. Twenty-one years before this event, Pope John Paul II was already anticipating that celebration and devoting himself to prepare the Church and the world for it. This forward-looking orientation is based on trust and confidence in the Holy Spirit guiding him and the whole Church into the future (2–3). It would carry on what Pope Paul VI, in *Ecclesiam Suam*, calls "the dialogue of salvation" both within the Church and with those outside her. This dialogue must proceed without triumphalism:

> In accordance with the example of her Master, who is "humble in heart," the Church also should have humility as her foundation. (4.1)

Linking his agenda with that of both Vatican II and the pontificate of Pope Paul VI, Pope John Paul II closes the encyclical's first chapter speaking of unity. This includes *unity within the Church* that "springs from the principle of collegiality" (5.1), and the quest for the restoration of *unity among the divided Christian churches* that was so much in the heart of Pope John XXIII. As Pope John Paul II exhorts us:

> We must therefore seek unity without being discouraged at the difficulties...otherwise we would be unfaithful to the word of Christ, we would fail to accomplish his testament. Have we the right to run this risk? (6.1)

COMMUNICATING THE MYSTERY OF THE REDEMPTION

In order that we may draw closer to the "everlasting Father" as the new millennium approaches we must look in only one direction: toward Christ, the Redeemer of man.

> The Church does not cease to listen to his words. She rereads them continually. With the greatest devotion she reconstructs every detail of his life…The Church never ceases to relive his death on the Cross and his Resurrection…[and] unceasingly celebrates the Eucharist, finding in it the "fountain of life and holiness." (7.4)

The challenge that the Pope sees is *how* to bring the mystery of Christ to peoples and individuals in our time, since this is the mission of the Church for all time and in all times. First, Christ must be proclaimed as the source of all good in the world, and as the one who has "reforged" the link between God and humanity that was broken by Adam's sin. He has become our reconciliation with the Father. Secondly, despite the technological progress of our age, as Vatican II's "Pastoral Constitution on the Church in the Modern World" (*Gaudium et Spes*) makes clear, people still struggle to understand the meaning of their existence. However,

> Christ, the Redeemer of the world, is the one who has penetrated…into the mystery of man and entered his "heart". Rightly, therefore does the Second Vatican Council teach: "The truth is that only in the mystery of the Incarnate Word does the mystery of man take on light…For, by his Incarnation, he, the Son of God, *in a certain way united himself with each man.*" (8.2; cf. *GS* 22)

In Jesus Christ, God himself has drawn near to us, and he remains with us through the gift of the "Spirit of Truth."

THE HUMAN DIMENSION
OF THE MYSTERY OF THE REDEMPTION

Pope John Paul II realizes that humanity needs more to understand Christ than a presentation of theological truths and principles. He says that, "Man cannot live without love." He must encounter and experience love. In order to discover God and even one's own self, one has to "draw near to Christ" and "enter into him" (10.1).

> If this profound process takes place within him, he then bears fruit not only of adoration of God but also of deep wonder at himself …
>
> In reality, the name for that deep amazement at man's worth and dignity is the Gospel…It is also called Christianity. (10.1–2)

The Holy Father understands that the full truth, both about God *and* about the dignity and worth of each human person, can only be fully attained by the one who knows and loves Jesus Christ.

THE MISSION OF THE CHURCH

The Second Vatican Council acknowledged the truths that are found in other world religions. Nonetheless, the Church has "the great mission of revealing Christ to the world, helping each person to find himself in Christ…and helping everyone to get to know 'the unsearchable riches of Christ' (Eph. 3:8)" (11.5). Every Christian must be a missionary modeled on Christ "the first evangelizer" (12.2). This mission must be carried out with a great respect for the freedom and dignity of each person. Christ is seen "as the one who brings man freedom based on truth" (12.3). He has come into the world to "bear witness to the truth" (Jn. 18:37), and he is himself "the way, and the truth, and the life" (Jn. 14:6).

REDEEMED MAN AND HIS SITUATION IN THE MODERN WORLD

This title of the third section of *Redemptor Hominis* summarizes concisely the unique approach of Pope John Paul II in this encyclical letter. He focuses on the *human person*—who finds himself and his dignity in Jesus Christ—and also on the situation, role and mission of this person, redeemed by Christ, in contemporary society.

The mission of the Church is expressed in profoundly "personalist" terms when the Holy Father says

> the Church wishes to serve this single end: that each person may be able to find Christ, in order that Christ may walk with each

person the path of life, with the power of the truth about man
and the world that is contained in the mystery of the Incarnation
and the Redemption and with the power of the love that is radi-
ated by that truth. (13.1)

The Church seeks to put each person "in touch" with the Redeemer, Jesus
Christ. At the same time, the Church has wide-ranging social concerns, as she
"cannot remain insensible to whatever serves man's true welfare, any more
than she can remain indifferent to what threatens it" (13.2). As the Holy Father
says, we are not dealing with "man" in the abstract, but in his real historical
circumstances. He notes how *Gaudium et Spes*, in its analysis of the modern
world, "always passed from the external elements of this situation to the truth
within humanity" (14.2). The Church, therefore, cannot speak about "the
world" without addressing the trials, struggles, hopes and joys of each person
in her endeavor "to make human life ever more human" (14.4) with the exemplar of that full humanity being Jesus Christ.

　　This is a great affirmation of the dignity and value of the human person, but it is also presented as a *challenge* to each person to live and act in a
way that befits and supports the true welfare of each person and of humanity
as a whole. For example, man cannot use the natural environment merely as
a "consumer" to exploit it, but must conserve its resources and preserve its
beauty for the good of all (cf. 15). John Paul II notes:

The development of technology and...contemporary civilization...demand a proportional development of morals and ethics.
For the present, this last development seems unfortunately to be
always left behind. (15.4)

Certainly the truly human and moral use of technological advances is
one of the greatest challenges of the present day. To be a Christian is to
pose prophetic questions:

whether in the context of this progress man, as man, is truly becoming better, that is to say more mature spiritually, more aware
of the dignity of his humanity, more responsible, more open to
others, especially the neediest and the weakest, and readier to
give and to aid all.

> This question must be put by Christians, precisely because Jesus
> Christ has made them so universally sensitive about the problem
> of man. (15.3–4)

The teaching of Pope John Paul II in this encyclical both echoes the teaching of Vatican II in *Gaudium et Spes*, which he helped author, and anticipates the social teaching of his later encyclicals including the concept of the "civilization of love" as a prophetic response to the "culture of death" that we see advancing (seemingly so inexorably) around us. In Chapter III the Holy Father also proclaims the reasons behind the Church's call to work for economic justice, for defense of human rights (including religious freedom), and for peace, that "comes down to respect for man's inviolable rights" (17.2).

THE CHURCH'S SPIRITUAL MISSION
AND HER PARTICIPATION IN CHRIST'S MINISTRY

Chapter III of *Redemptoris Hominis* leaves no doubt about the intense involvement of the Christian in the affairs of the world out of concern for the good of the person and the common good of society. Chapter IV makes it equally clear that the reason and the strength for such involvement comes from the mystery of Jesus, who through his Incarnation and Redemption has made us new creatures (cf. 2 Cor. 5:17). "Christ's union with man is power and the source of power" (18.2). The Holy Spirit is also the power that unites the Church and provides her with the powers (cf. Rom. 15:13; 1 Cor. 1:24), gifts (cf. Is. 11:2–3; Acts 2:38) and fruits (cf. Gal. 5:22–23) to carry out her mission in the world. Hence, Pope John Paul exhorts us to cry out, "Come Holy Spirit! Come! Come!" and observes, "This appeal to the Spirit…is the answer to all the 'materialisms' of our age" (18.3–4). The Church is not alone in recognizing the great spiritual hunger in our time. Others, including non-Christians, know and seek to respond to this hunger. Yet, it is only through the mystery of Christ and grace of the Holy Spirit that people will receive that "divine adoption" making them daughters and sons of God and thus truly satisfying humanity's deepest longing.

SHARING IN CHRIST'S MISSION

Besides imparting new spiritual life, the grace of Christ also enables God's children to serve as Christ served, sharing in Christ's "triple office as priest, as prophet and as king" (18.4). Vatican II's *Lumen Gentium* accentuated the teaching that *all* in the Church share in Christ's three-fold ministry, *not* just the clergy and religious. In this encyclical letter Pope John Paul II highlights certain aspects of each of these ministries.

Concerning the "prophetic" office, he notes that while the *Magisterium* of the Church has primary responsibility for safeguarding and proclaiming divine truth, the Catholic theologian is to be closely allied *with the Magisterium* in the mission of teaching the truth, never viewing theology as "a simple collection of his own personal ideas" (19.4). The Pope also stresses the importance of catechesis, "beginning with the fundamental field, family catechesis, that is the catechesis by parents of their children" (19.6). The encyclical's section on catechesis anticipates the publication of "On Catechesis in Our Time" (*Catechesi Tradendae*) later in the same year.

Regarding our participation in Christ's priestly office, the Holy Father focuses on the Eucharist. The Pope's statements on the Eucharist are powerful; and in the "year of the Eucharist," which he initiated, they were especially meaningful:

> The Eucharist is the center and summit of the whole sacramental life, through which each Christian receives the saving power of the Redemption...the entire sacramental life of the Church and of each Christian reaches its summit and fullness in the Eucharist. (20.1)

> Nevertheless, it is certain that the Church of the new Advent, the Church that is continually preparing for the new coming of the Lord, must be the Church of the Eucharist and of Penance. Only when viewed in this spiritual aspect of her life and activity is she seen to be the Church of the divine mission, the Church *in statu missionis* ["in the state of mission"], as the Second Vatican Council has shown her to be. (20.8)

Penance or Reconciliation is the sacrament that expresses and brings about the continual conversion of heart that is always important for the Christian and necessary to approach the Lord in the Sacrament of the Eucharist.

Sharing in the "kingly" mission of Christ "is truly possible only by 'being a servant'" (21.1). To carry out this kingly mission, the Holy Father stresses, requires human and spiritual maturity. It means hearing and responding to one's particular vocation, one's call from God, and living that vocation faithfully, as either a married person, single person, priest or religious. By being faithful and serving the Lord in one's personal vocation, the Church is built up and its mission is effectively extended.

MARY

The final section of the Holy Father's first encyclical letter (as is the case in all of his encyclicals and other documents) is devoted to Mary, "the mother in whom we trust" (22.1). Referring to *Lumen Gentium*'s final chapter on Mary and Pope Paul VI's declaration of Mary as "Mother of the Church," Pope John Paul reflects on her essential role in God's plan of redemption. "We can say that the mystery of the Redemption took shape beneath the heart of the Virgin of Nazareth when she pronounced her 'fiat'" (22.4). Mary is also praised for being exceptionally close to each person and all that happens to him or her. This is a mother's role, and it is a model for the maternal care and love that the Church and her members are to have for each person. Through Mary's intercession, joined with the prayer of the whole Church in this season of a "new Advent," Pope John Paul II finally expresses his hope "that through this prayer we shall be able to receive the Holy Spirit coming upon us (cf. Acts 1:8) and thus become Christ's witnesses 'to the end of the earth'" (22.6).

Pope John Paul II began his pontificate "starting from Christ" the Redeemer and looking forward to the new millennium, which lay ahead. Is it mere coincidence that twenty-one years later, in the year 2001, Pope John Paul included a chapter "Starting Afresh from Christ" in his letter for the beginning of the third millennium? I think not:

> We shall not be saved by a formula but by a Person, and the assurance which he gives us: *I am with you!*
>
> It is not therefore a matter of inventing a "new program". The program already exists: it is the plan found in the Gospel and in the living Tradition, it is the same as ever. Ultimately, it has its center in Christ himself, who is to be known, loved and imitated, so that in him we may live the life of the Trinity, and with him transform history until its fulfillment in the heavenly Jerusalem...

This program for all times is our program for the Third Millennium. (*NMI* 29.2–3)

——————————— QUESTIONS FOR REFLECTION ———————————

1. "Through the Incarnation God gave human life the dimension that he intended [humanity] to have from his first beginning" (*RH* 1). What is that dimension? How did God, through the Incarnation, restore this dimension to humanity?

2. What important "themes" of Pope John Paul II's pontificate are found in his first encyclical, *Redemptor Hominis*?

3. Discuss the various ways that the life of the Church and the life of Christians focus on Jesus Christ. How, practically, can the Church meet the challenge of bringing the mystery of Christ to peoples and individuals in *our* time who do not know him?

4. What is the importance of Jesus Christ in bringing people today to recognize the dignity and inestimable value of each human person? How is this concept of the dignity of the human person central to the Church's "social teaching" (i.e. working for justice, peace, and human rights)?

5. How can the message of this encyclical letter answer the great "spiritual hunger" and the search for meaning that we experience in our times?

6. How is the Church called to share in and extend the *mission* of Jesus Christ today? Why are the Eucharist and Mary essential in helping us to know Jesus and to carry out his mission in the world?

FOR FURTHER READING

- Second Vatican Council, Pastoral Constitution on the Church in the Modern World (*Gaudium et Spes*)
- *Catechism*, 849–856 (Mission); 512–521 (Christ); 355–361 (Man)
- *Compendium*, 359
- Pope Benedict XVI, *Jesus of Nazareth*
- Romano Guardini, *The Lord*
- Peter Kreeft, *Between Heaven and Hell*
- Ignace de la Potterie, S.J., *The Hour of Jesus*
- Alan Schreck, *Jesus: What Catholics Believe*
- Donald Senior, *Jesus: A Gospel Portrait*
- Frank Sheed, *To Know Christ Jesus*

2

Dives in Misericordia
"Rich in Mercy"

The Second Encyclical Letter of Pope John Paul II

November 30, 1980

Following his first encyclical letter on Christ, "The Redeemer of Man" (*Redemptor Hominis*), released the prior year, Pope John Paul II issued a companion encyclical focusing on God who is "rich in mercy." This encyclical letter is a companion or a continuation of *Redemptor Hominis* in that both letters are focused on God's relationship with us, his human creatures. While *Redemptor Hominis* focuses on Jesus Christ as the prototype, the "first-born," of redeemed humanity and the savior of the human race, *Dives in Misericordia* looks at Christ as the manifestation and revealer of God the Father's great love for man, which is expressed consummately as mercy. Pope John Paul also discusses possible misunderstandings of mercy and the relationship between mercy and justice. His primary task, though, is to exalt God for his mercy towards the human race and to exhort all who are recipients of God's mercy to show mercy to others and continually to pray for God's mercy to be lavished upon the world.

SEEING THE FATHER

Dives in Misericordia is divided into eight chapters. I will highlight some of the main themes of each. A number of times throughout this encyclical, the Pope explains that the primary task of his pontificate is to implement the doctrine of the Second Vatican Council. This encyclical letter is particularly an unfolding and application of Vatican II's "Pastoral Constitution on the Church in the Modern World" (*Gaudium et Spes*), which refutes the false dichotomy between spiritual life (*serving God*) and life and activity in the world (*serving man*). *Dives in Misericordia* begins by considering that the Son of God both revealed the Father and showed his love for the Father (*served the Father*) by becoming human and, in that condition, loved and served those around him, especially the poor and those in need. Thus we learn that in serving other people in and through Christ, we are at the same time and by the same action serving God. God desires us to seek the betterment of the human condition and to confirm and defend human dignity. In doing so, we are offering fitting service and a pleasing sacrifice to God.

Jesus, through his words and works, is the incarnation of mercy: "*He himself, in a certain sense, is mercy.* To the person who sees it [mercy] in him— and finds it in him—God becomes 'visible' in a particular way as the Father 'who is rich in mercy' (Eph. 2:4)" (2.2; emphasis mine). As Jesus reveals God as the "Father of mercies," Pope John Paul observes that due to the myriad of difficult situations in the Church and the world today many people "are turning, I would say almost spontaneously, to the mercy of God" (2.5). Certainly our faith teaches us not just to meditate abstractly on the concept of mercy, but also to call upon the "Father of mercies" in the name of Christ and in union with him (cf. 2.7).

THE MESSIANIC MESSAGE
AND ITS PREFIGUREMENT IN THE OLD TESTAMENT

The second and third chapters of *Dives in Misericordia* explore the testimony of the Sacred Scriptures to the mercy of God. Chapter II continues to focus on Jesus Christ as the embodiment of God's mercy, making the Father present by his actions and words. From the beginning of his public ministry Jesus speaks of his messianic mission of proclaiming the good news to the poor (cf. Lk. 4:18–19), and his mighty works were a testimony that he had been sent by the Father (cf. Lk. 7:22–23). "Making the Father present as love and mercy is, in Christ's own consciousness, the fundamental touchstone of his mission as the Messiah" (3.4). Also, the mercy of God was one of the principal themes of Jesus' parables and preaching, such as in the parables of the Good Samaritan (Lk. 10:30–37), the Prodigal Son (Lk. 15:11–32), the Good Shepherd (Mt. 18:12–14), and even the Merciless Servant (Mt. 18:23–27). It is also seen in

Jesus' preaching of the great commandment (Mt. 22:37–38) and the Beatitudes (Mt. 5:7: "Blessed are the merciful, for they shall obtain mercy"). Hence, Jesus both reveals the mercy of God in his actions and shows "that call to mercy which is one of the essential elements of the Gospel ethos" (3.7).

Jesus' messianic ministry, of course, is the culmination of the mercy of God shown throughout the Old Testament (Chapter III). Time and again God's people violated the covenant relationship, and individuals (like David) fell into personal sin, but whenever they cried out to God they received mercy. God solemnly declared to Moses that he was a "God merciful and gracious, slow to anger, and abounding in steadfast love and faithfulness" (Ex. 34:6).

But what about this justice of God in punishing sin? The Holy Father explains that while justice and mercy are sometimes contrasted, they are not opposed. Mercy is a particular expression of God's love. Because God lovingly created the human race and desires every human person to come into union with him (presently and for eternity), his love is always ready to forgive sin, which is mercy:

> Love is "greater" than justice: greater in the sense that it is primary and fundamental. Love, so to speak, conditions justice and, in the final analysis, justice serves love. The primacy and superiority of love vis-à-vis justice—this is a mark of the whole of revelation—are revealed precisely through mercy. (4.11; cf. Ps. 40:11, 98:2–3; Is. 45:21, 51:5, 8; 56:1)

Later in the encyclical the Holy Father explains further that nowhere does forgiveness (or mercy as its source) "mean indulgence towards evil, towards scandals, towards injury or insult" and that "reparation for evil and scandal, compensation for injury, and satisfaction for insult are conditions for forgiveness" (14.10). Pope John Paul concludes:

> Thus the fundamental structure of justice always enters into the sphere of mercy. Mercy, however, has the power to confer on justice a new content, which is expressed most simply and fully in forgiveness. (14.11)

THE PARABLE OF THE PRODIGAL SON

For many (including myself), the "heart" of this encyclical is Pope John Paul's elucidation of the parable of the prodigal son. It exemplifies how forgiveness is central to mercy, and how justice is not sufficient to express the attitude of God the Father toward his children, as seen in the figure of the father in the parable to his prodigal son. In justice, the son should have been accepted back into his own father's house as a hired servant, as he understood. This certainly would have been "a great humiliation and source of shame" (5.5). The son had not only squandered his inheritance but he had hurt and offended his father by his conduct, and he was ashamed of it. Pope John Paul astutely observes that we must have an "exact picture of the prodigal son's state of mind...to understand exactly what the mercy of God consists in" (6.1).

The father of the parable is "faithful to his fatherhood, faithful to the love that he had always lavished on his son" (6.1). He not only welcomes the "lost" son home but is also filled with joy and calls for a feast. The joy of the father overcomes the shame of the son.

This is critically important because today many reject the concept of mercy as being degrading or demeaning to the one who receives it. True mercy respects the dignity of the person. The father realizes that his son has been "saved" by his return, and he rejoices because he loves the son. As Pope John Paul comments:

> Mercy—as Christ has presented it in the parable of the prodigal son—has the interior form of love that in the New Testament is called agape. This love is able to reach down to every prodigal son, to every human misery, and above all to every form of moral misery, to sin. When this happens, the person who is the object of mercy does not feel humiliated, but rather found again and "restored to value." (6.3)

Rather than offending human dignity, mercy restores human dignity by revealing to the person the full truth about himself: that despite his struggle or failure, he is forgiven, loved, and accepted by God and by others who act in mercy. This realization by a person is also an experience of conversion, which is "the most concrete expression of the working of love and of the presence of mercy in the human world" (6.5). As the Holy Father concludes this chapter, mercy is manifested in its true and proper aspect when it restores to value, promotes and draws good from all forms of evil existing in the world and in man [cf. Rom. 12:21]…Mercy constitutes the fundamental content of the messianic message of Christ and the constitutive power of his mission. (6.5)

THE PASCHAL MYSTERY AND MERCY

The greatest sign of God's mercy is Jesus Christ's total gift of himself for the salvation of the human race by his death on Calvary, and his Resurrection to new life on Easter Sunday. This Paschal Mystery shows that God did not only love the human race initially in creating us, but "also grants participation in the very life of God: Father, Son, and Holy Spirit" (7.4). By his death, Jesus both fulfilled the demands of justice, which requires reparation for all the sins of the human race, and radically reveals God's mercy in forgiving the whole history of human offenses against his goodness.

But the mercy of God does not end either at the Cross or through our restoration to life in the Resurrection. "Christ's messianic program, the program of mercy, becomes the program of his people, the program of the Church" (8.3). The Church carries out what Mary proclaimed in her "Magnificat": that the Lord's mercy extends "from generation to generation" (Lk. 1:50). This is the subject of the sixth chapter of *Dives in Misericordia*, which (following *Gaudium et Spes*) begins by examining the hopes and problems of the present day that spring from new developments (scientific, technological, economic, etc.). Pope John Paul concludes that there is a growing sense of uneasiness and unrest in the world, and remorse over the ever-widening gap between the affluent and the poor. To meet these needs, the Holy Father says that "justice alone is not enough," and can even be destructive if not supplemented by "that deeper power, which is love" (12.3). The Church must "bear witness in her whole mission to God's mercy" (Ch. XII, Intro.), by professing it and seeking to make it incarnate. Pope John Paul II writes:

The Church lives an authentic life when she professes and proclaims mercy—the most stupendous attribute of the Creator and of the Redeemer—and when she brings people close to the sources of the Savior's mercy, of which she is the trustee and dispenser. (13.3)

These sources are "constant meditation on the Word of God and above all conscious and mature participation in the Eucharist and in the Sacrament of Penance or Reconciliation" (13.3). Drawing from these sources, both individuals and the whole Church are called to practice mercy towards others (cf. 14.1), to make mercy a lifestyle (cf. 14.2) with the crucified Christ as "the loftiest model, inspiration and encouragement" (14.3). It is through the giving and receiving of mercy that there grows a sense of equality between people whether we are giving or receiving mercy, of which we all have need. This "exchange of mercy," if it becomes widespread, has the power to bring about what Pope Paul VI first termed the "civilization of love" (14.7). We pray for this when we say "thy Kingdom come." For God's kingdom or the "civilization of love" to be realized, mercy cannot be something we extend only to the poor or to criminals or notable sinners. Rather, "merciful love is supremely indispensable between those who are closest to one another: between husbands and wives, between parents and children, between friends; and it is indispensable in education and in pastoral work" (14.6). (One is reminded of St. John Bosco, who was known for his emphasis on kindness, an expression of mercy, in teaching the faith to the young.) Thus the extension of mercy and unlimited forgiveness, in and through Christ, is an intrinsic part of the Church's mission. It is a powerful force both to humanize and to sanctify the world.

THE PRAYER OF THE CHURCH IN OUR TIMES

The final chapter of *Dives in Misericordia* reminds us that in our age, in which modern man often "lacks the courage to utter the word 'mercy'" (15.2), it is even more necessary for the Church to speak of God's mercy and to continually and fervently pray for it to be manifested in the world. This message of mercy is evident not only in John Paul's words, but in his life and actions. In 1997, Pope John Paul II made a pilgrimage to the tomb of Sr. Faustina, who received the message of Divine Mercy from Jesus in 1931. There the Holy Father declared that "the message of Divine Mercy has always been near and dear to me...In a sense it forms the image of my Pontificate." Then in 2000, he canonized Sr. Faustina and decreed through the Congregation for Divine Worship that "throughout the world the Second Sunday of Easter will receive the name Divine Mercy Sunday, a perennial invitation to the Christian world to face, with confidence in divine benevolence, the difficulties and trials that mankind will experience in the years to come" (May 23, 2000). Like St. Faustina before him, Pope John Paul II points to Mary as the Mother of Mercy, who proclaimed God's mercy "from generation to generation."

At the end of *Dives in Misericordia*, the Holy Father exhorts the Church to earnestly pray, with Mary and the saints, "that the love which is in the Father may once again be revealed at this stage in history, and that, through the work of the Son and Holy Spirit, it may be shown to be present in our modern world and to be more powerful than evil: more powerful than sin and death" (15.6).

───────── QUESTIONS FOR REFLECTION ─────────

1. How does this encyclical letter resolve the apparent opposition between the spiritual life ("serving God") and working for good in the world ("serving humanity")? Explore how Jesus, who is the "incarnation of mercy" or simply "mercy" (himself) resolves this apparent conflict.

2. How does Pope John Paul II explain the relationship of justice and mercy, so that these are not seen as opposed? Why is love "greater" than justice?

3. How is forgiveness related to—and a necessary expression of—mercy?

4. How is Jesus' parable of the "prodigal son" an ideal expression of God's mercy?

5. Reflect on this statement, based on the teaching of this encyclical letter: "Mercy restores human dignity by revealing to the person the full truth about himself: that despite his failure he is forgiven, loved and accepted by God and by others who act in mercy."

6. Why is the paschal mystery of Jesus the greatest sign of God's mercy?

7. How does the Church proclaim and carry out Christ's "mission of mercy"? Why is it not sufficient for the Church to seek and demand justice in the world?

8. What are the wellsprings of mercy that enable the Church to make mercy a "lifestyle" and build a "civilization of love"?

FOR FURTHER READING

- Fr. George Kosicki, *John Paul II: The Great Mercy Pope*
- Henri Nouwen, *A Cry for Mercy: Prayers from the Genesee*
- Henri Nouwen, *The Return of the Prodigal Son*
- Vatican II, Pastoral Constitution on the Church in the Modern World (*Gaudium et Spes*)
- *Catechism*, 210–227 (Father); 1322–1405 (Eucharist); 1422–1470 (Reconciliation)

3

Laborem Exercens
"On Human Work"

The Third Encyclical Letter of Pope John Paul II

September 14, 1981

Pope John Paul II's first social encyclical, *Laborem Exercens* ("On Human Work"), extended a modern papal tradition of publishing social encyclicals on the anniversary of the first great social encyclical, *Rerum Novarum* of Pope Leo XIII.

The ninetieth anniversary of that first social encyclical came at a time when the world socio-economic order was dominated by communist nations in which the government controlled the means of production, by wealthy and largely capitalist nations seeking to expand their wealth and influence, and by a wide range of economically underdeveloped and developing nations seeking a path to stability, growth and prosperity. In a later encyclical letter, *Sollicitudo Rei Socialis*, Pope John Paul addressed the unique opportunities and challenges of each of these. In *Laborem Exercens* he examines one aspect that they share in common: work and its meaning for human persons.

DIGNITY OF THE PERSON

The key to understanding work, for Pope John Paul II, is to understand the person who works. He developed a distinctive Christian anthropology—a Christian understanding of the nature of humanity. One much-discussed aspect of this is his "theology of the body." In this encyclical he describes what he calls the "gospel of work" (7.1; cf. 6.5). What is the meaning of work for the Christian? It is only to be rightly understood if we see each person, each worker, as created and loved by God and thus possessing the dignity of a son or a daughter of God, destined to eternal life. Thus, the essential meaning of work is not determined by *what* work is done (the *objective* meaning of work—i.e. what is the *object* or *goal* of the work), but by *who* does the work: a person (who gives work its *subjective* meaning). Preserving the dignity and fostering the welfare of the person who works (the *worker*) is central to the thought of Pope John Paul II. We recall this section from Vatican II's "Pastoral Constitution on the Church in the Modern World" (*Gaudium et Spes*, 34–35), teaching that the dignity of the person is central to the meaning of work.

Human activity proceeds from man: it is also ordered to him. When he works, not only does he transform matter and society, but he also fulfills himself. He learns, he develops his faculties, and he emerges from and transcends himself. Rightly understood, this kind of growth is more precious than any kind of wealth that can be amassed. It is what a man is, rather than what he has, that counts. Technical progress is of less value than advances towards greater justice, wider brotherhood, and a more humane social environment (cf. *GS* 35).

WORK: CURSE OR BLESSING?

Our human experience of the drudgery and even the pain of work may lead us to consider work not as *humanizing*, but as the Book of Genesis indicates, a *curse*—punishment for the sin of our first parents and for all subsequent sins. Although the necessity of work is a consequence of the Fall (original sin), Pope John Paul II stresses the virtue and value of work. Indeed, the Sacred Scripture testifies to this when the Lord commands the first parents to "fill the earth and subdue it" (Gen. 1:28) and to have dominion over it and all creatures. Through work, humanity acts with God to order and bring forth the goodness and potential of the earth, and develops strength, discipline and character in the process. Rather than being *dehumanizing*, "these actions must all serve to realize his humanity" (6.2). As John Paul continues:

> Work is a good thing for man…because through work **man not only transforms nature**, adapting it to his own needs, but he also *achieves fulfillment* **as a human** being and indeed, in a sense becomes "more a human being".

Without this consideration it is impossible to understand
the meaning of the virtue of industriousness. (9.3–4; bolded
emphasis mine)

The highest exemplar of this is Jesus Christ who "devoted most of the years of
his life on earth to *manual work* at the carpenter's bench" (6.5) and his last years
to the great work of proclaiming and establishing God's kingdom. Pope John
Paul remarks that Jesus' labor "constitutes in itself the most eloquent 'Gospel of
work', showing that the basis for determining the value of human work is not
primarily the kind of work being done but the fact that the one who is doing it
is a person" (6.5). As a result, we can no longer divide people into "classes" and
judge their value as persons according to the kind of work they do, since "*the
primary basis of the value of work is man himself*, who is its subject" (6.6).

On this basis, the Pope insists that the worker can never be viewed or
treated primarily as a mere instrument or means of production. Historically,
this abuse led to "the impetuous emergence of a great burst of solidarity between workers, first and foremost industrial workers." This movement of
solidarity among workers was a "reaction *against the degradation of man as the
subject of work*, and against the unheard-of accompanying exploitation in the
fields of wages, working conditions, and social security for the worker" (8.2).
Many point to John Paul II's undisguised support of the Polish workers' movement called *Solidarity* as a significant factor of the downfall of communism in
his native land, and eventually to the end of the communist domination of
Eastern Europe in 1989.

Yet *Laborem Exercens* does not dwell on the past. It calls for a new and
deeper analysis of the situation of the worker and of work in the present age
of technological advancement. It urges an informed Catholic laity to tackle
new problems created by technology (such as unemployment or shifts in employment needs) and by the spread of industrialization (such as diminishing
natural resources and environmental pollution).

Nor does the Holy Father consider only the *personal* meaning and benefit of work. He also considers two other spheres of work: its relation to family
life and to society. "Work constitutes a foundation for the formation of *family
life*" (10.1) in two ways: first, it provides a means of subsistence "which man
normally gains through work," and secondly, "work and industriousness" are
part of the process of education in the family, in that work is one factor in

becoming a full human being and "becoming a human being is precisely the main purpose of the whole process of education" (10.1). Hence, "the family is simultaneously a *community made possible by work* and the first *school of work*, within the house, for every person" (10.2).

Regarding *society*, the Holy Father observes that the cumulative result of the work of individuals and families is the creation of a culture and a society, which is "a great historical and social incarnation of the work of all generations" (10.3).

THE CONFLICT BETWEEN LABOR AND CAPITAL

In this encyclical, Pope John Paul II desired to "catechize" the faithful in some of the basic principles of Catholic social teaching, which first had been presented in a modern context in *Rerum Novarum*. In the third section of *Laborem Exercens*, he exposes the false dichotomy between *capital* and *labor*. Capital can mean either of two things:

1. The resources of the earth, which are God's gifts that have been made accessible and useable through human work (labor) (12.3)

2. The means of production, or products or money generated by these means of production, which are all, in some way, the fruit of human labor (12.4)

The Catholic Church has always taught "*the principle of the priority of labor over capital*" (12.1), since no *capital* would exist without labor (human work) and it is an instrument used by those who work. Stated in another way, John Paul II says that through his work a person "*enters into two inheritances*": the inheritance of nature (given to all) and the inheritance of "what others have already developed on the basis of these resources" (13.2).

Of course, historically the struggle has been over the ownership of these "inheritances," either natural resources or means of production. The Church continues to teach a right of private property (and hence private ownership of *capital*), but only when it is understood that "*the right to private property is subordinated to the right of common use*, to the fact that goods are meant for everyone" (14.2). Likewise, Pope John Paul accepts that there could be an acceptable *socialization* (or "social ownership") of capital, but only when the worker has access to this and thus reaps the benefits of his own work (resulting in a sense of working "for oneself" and not just for others or for the collective).

In a beautiful image, Pope John Paul II expresses that this goal is achieved "when on the basis of his work each worker is fully entitled to consider himself a part-owner of the great workbench at which he is working with everyone else. A way toward that goal could be found by associating labor with the ownership of capital, as far as possible" (14.7). I have witnessed this when a number of years ago a local steel mill, instead of merging or closing, sold shares of the company to its workers, thus saving the company and giving the workers a real investment in their own future.

THE RIGHTS OF WORKERS

The fourth section of *Laborem Exercens* reviews the rights of workers. Space does not permit a development of all Pope John Paul's themes here, so only a few original contributions will be mentioned. First, the Holy Father distinguishes between the *direct employers* of workers, and those whom he calls *indirect employers*: those who have some responsibility for workers' status and rights because of their influence on economic, social, legal and political conditions that affect workers. The first and most influential *indirect employer* is the State, which "must conduct a just labor policy" (17.2). Banks, conglomerates, multi-national corporations and the like also have tremendous influence on the condition of employment (such as wages) of workers whom they do not directly employ. Their decisions often dictate where and what type of work is available. "Overall planning," "international collaboration," "coordination" and room for "initiative" are all necessary for the rights of workers to be preserved and their needs to be rightly met in the complexity of today's global community (cf. 18.2–3).

Secondly, Pope John Paul II calls for some radical innovations in the social order with regard to work. Justice for workers, he argues, would include "a *family wage*—that is, a single salary given to the head of the family for his work, sufficient for the needs of the family without the other spouse having to take up gainful employment outside the home—or through *other social measures* such as family allowances of grants to mothers devoting themselves exclusively to the families" (19.3). This is related to the Pope's call for "a *social reevaluation of the mother's role*" that would protect her essential role in the family, which is the basic cell of society (19.4). (It should be noted that the encyclical also insists that women should not be discriminated against nor be excluded from jobs for which they are capable.) Nonetheless, "the *true advancement of women* requires that labor should be structured in such a way that women do not have to pay for their advancement by abandoning what is specific to them and at the expense of the family" (19.5).

Other topics treated in this section include the importance of unions to preserve workers' rights, the dignity of agricultural work, the special needs of disabled persons, and challenges and questions concerning immigrants in search of work.

ELEMENTS OF A SPIRITUALITY OF WORK

A final and original contribution of this encyclical letter regards "*a spirituality of work*" (24.2). This spirituality is based in God's revelation that "*man*, created in the image of God, *shares by his work in the activity of the Creator*" (25.2). The "Book of Genesis, is also *in a sense the first 'gospel of work'*," in that it speaks both of work as a sharing in God's creative power, and of the weekly rest from work. This weekly rest allows time to focus on and prepare for our final goal—the eternal rest that we hope to have with God in eternity when our work in this world is done (25.3). (See also Pope John Paul II's Apostolic Letter, *Dies Domini*, "On Keeping the Lord's Day Holy.")

The "spirituality of work" also teaches that we are sanctified by our work, even "*the most ordinary everyday activities*" (25.4). This spirituality requires the *maturity* to realize that what we accomplish through our work is not just our achievement but also "a sign of God's greatness and the flowering of his own mysterious design" (25.5; cf. *GS* 34). Further, by participating actively and properly in the work of this world, Christians will permeate it with "the Spirit of Christ and more effectively achieve its purpose in justice, charity and peace" (25.6; cf. *LG* 36).

Pope John Paul brings this "spirituality of work" to a climax in his reflections on the New Testament revelation. St. Paul often points to the importance of work and urges Christians to undertake it for the Lord, with a proper attitude. Although Jesus does not address the issue of work as directly, Pope John Paul highlights his many parables of work and workers, including women, and observes that Jesus "was himself a man of work" who "*looks with love upon human work* and the different forms it takes, seeing in each one of these forms a particular facet of man's likeness with God, the Creator and

Father" (26.1). As the Second Vatican Council taught, work is not only necessary for the fulfillment of God's plan for the earth (such as progress and development), but it benefits the person: "For when a man works he not only alters things and society, he develops himself as well. He learns much, he cultivates his resources; he goes outside of himself and beyond himself. Rightly understood, this kind of growth is of greater value than any external riches which can be garnered" (26.5; *GS* 35).

However, there is an "invisible" aspect of the spirituality of work that is even more profound. The work of Jesus Christ was brought to completion in the Paschal Mystery, which "contains *the Cross* of Christ and his obedience unto death" and leads to "*the Resurrection* with the power of the Holy Spirit" (27.2). The spirituality of work is caught up in this mystery. "The Christian finds in human work a small part of the Cross of Christ and accepts it in the same spirit of redemption in which Christ accepted his Cross for us" (27.5). In this work is found not only the suffering of toil, but "a *glimmer* of new life, of the *new good*, as if it were an announcement of the 'new heaven and the new earth' (cf. 2 Pt. 3:13; Rev. 21:1) in which man and the world participate precisely through the toil that goes with work" (27.5).

In human work there is a *glimmer* of the Resurrection, of that "'new earth' [2 Pt. 3:13] where justice dwells" (27.6), for which we wait in hope. As Pope John Paul II concludes:

> Let the Christian who listens to the word of the living God, uniting work with prayer, know the place that his work has not only in *earthly progress* but also in *the development of the Kingdom of God*, to which we are all called through the power of the Holy Spirit and through the word of the Gospel. (27.8)

―――――――――― QUESTIONS FOR REFLECTION ――――――――――

1. In order to understand the true meaning of human labor or work, why is it necessary to begin with a proper and correct understanding of the human person?

2. What are the benefits of suitable work to the person doing it?

3. Is work a curse or punishment? What has overcome the "negative" aspects of human work?

4. Why is it important to vigilantly guard against the ways work can become degrading or unnecessarily harmful to those who work? Has the Catholic Church taken a stand against the harmful or abusive effects of work? If so, how?

5. What is the meaning of "capital" in this encyclical? What is meant by the priority of labor over capital, which the Catholic Church teaches?

6. Who are "indirect" employers? Why is it important that just practices regarding workers be observed both by direct and indirect employers?

7. What are some innovations or changes in the social order that Pope John Paul suggests to make work more just and humane?

8. Discuss the meaning of a "spirituality of work" and some elements or characteristics of such a spirituality.

FOR FURTHER READING

- Fr. Austin Fagothey, S.J., *Right and Reason*, Chapters 29 (Property), 31 (Work)
- Pope Leo XIII, On Capital and Labor (*Rerum Novarum*)
- Pope John Paul II, On Social Concerns (*Sollicitudo Rei Socialis*)
- Pope John Paul II, On the Centenary of *Rerum Novarum* (*Centesimus Annus*)
- *Catechism,* 2419–2449 (The Social Doctrine of the Church); 374–379 (Man in Paradise)

4

Slavorum Apostoli
"On Sts. Cyril and Methodius"

The Fourth Encyclical Letter of Pope John Paul II

June 2, 1985

Among the fourteen encyclical letters of Pope John Paul II, this one is unique. It commemorates the two great "apostles of the Slavic people," Sts. Cyril and Methodius (their religious names). Pope John Paul took the occasion of the eleventh centenary of the death of St. Methodius in 885 to call attention to their important contribution to the Church, to the Slavic people and to European culture. Of course, John Paul II was the first pope of Slavic descent, but that is not his primary reason for writing. He views these saints as great evangelizers, who were not afraid to leave their homeland in response to God's call and out of zeal for spreading the Gospel of Jesus Christ. They were also master catechists—tireless in their teaching of the faith among the people to whom they were sent.

THE PURPOSE OF THIS ENCYCLICAL LETTER

It may seem unusual that Pope John Paul II would honor the memory of these two saints by writing an encyclical letter: a universal letter to the Church of the highest authority and solemnity. He already had declared Sts. Cyril and Methodius Co-patrons of Europe (with St. Benedict) five years earlier in an apostolic letter, *Egregiae Virtutis.*

Why did Pope John Paul consider it important enough to promulgate an encyclical letter? The reason is that the life and mission of these saints exemplify characteristics that are of great importance for the Church today that are expressed vividly in the teaching of the Second Vatican Council. These characteristics are missionary zeal, an appreciation of different cultures, the catholicity or universality of the Church, and an unwavering commitment to the unity of the Church, expressed today in the movement to restore Christian unity (ecumenism). All of these prominent themes of Vatican II are powerfully manifest in the lives of Sts. Cyril and Methodius.

BIOGRAPHY

Before exploring these themes, John Paul II devotes Chapter II to a biographical sketch of the lives of these saints. These men initially lived in the Greek-speaking Byzantine region ruled by the Byzantine Emperor and the Patriarch of Constantinople. Cyril (Constantine) was a gifted scholar and teacher, known as "the Philosopher," and his elder brother Methodius was a monk who served on missions of church diplomacy. Cyril refused a brilliant political future to serve the Church, and eventually joined his older brother in the monastic life.

The brothers' lives changed forever when Prince Ratislav of Greater Moravia asked the Byzantine Emperor to send his peoples "a Bishop and teacher...able to explain to them the true Christian faith in their own language" (5.1). The emperor asked the brothers, who responded with faith and apostolic fervor. They took with them the Sacred Scriptures and the liturgical books "which they had...translated into the Old Slavonic language and written in a new alphabet, devised by Constantine [Cyril] the Philosopher" (5.2).

Pope John Paul points out that the brothers experienced many difficulties in their mission field, including the resistance of Latin clergy who refused to accept them and their 'vernacular' liturgy. Thus, they went to Rome, where Pope Hadrian II warmly received them and approved their Slavonic liturgical books. Sadly, Constantine became gravely ill and took the religious name Cyril shortly before he died on February 14, 869 (their feast day).

Methodius was consecrated by the Pope as Archbishop of Pannonia and made a papal legate. However, the political situation in the area grew worse and after his return to Moravia Methodius was imprisoned for two years, until the Pope (now John VIII) personally intervened to free him. Upon his return to Rome in 880, Pope John defended Methodius' orthodoxy and confirmed the validity of the Slavonic liturgy. Methodius returned to Constantinople in

881 or 882 where the Byzantine Emperor and patriarch also confirmed his authority among the Slavic people and his orthodoxy. Now at the end of his life, Methodius continued to translate important texts into Slavonic until his death in AD 885.

Having sketched the life of these holy brothers, John Paul II discusses the significance of their lives for the Church then and today.

HERALDS OF THE GOSPEL

One of the prominent themes of Vatican II is the importance of the missionary activity of the Church, as expressed in "The Decree on the Church's Missionary Activity" (*Ad Gentes*). The "new Springtime" that Pope John Paul II saw emerging in the Church is marked by a renewed missionary effort, outlined late in his 1990 encyclical letter *Redemptoris Missio* ("The Mission of the Redeemer"). Sts. Cyril and Methodius exemplified this missionary spirit as they gave up their contemplative life to become missionaries. As Constantine (Cyril) told the Emperor: "However tired and physically worn out I am, I will go with joy to that land; with joy I depart for the sake of the Christian faith" (9.1).

Their missionary endeavors were impressive not on account of the number of converts nor the physical hardships they endured. Rather, in the face of misunderstanding, severe criticism, "and even, for Saint Methodius, imprisonment accepted for love of Christ" (10.1), they brought the Gospel to the Slavic peoples in their own language and with no trace of superiority. Pope John Paul calls them "true models for all missionaries who in every period have accepted St. Paul's invitation to become all things to all people in order to redeem all" (11.2, cf. 1 Cor. 9:22). They "did not seek to impose on the peoples assigned to their preaching either the undeniable superiority of the Greek language and the Byzantine culture, or the customs and way of life of the more advanced society in which they had grown up" (13.1).

In their translations of the liturgical texts to the Slavonic language and in their warm embrace of the Slavic people and their culture, they are "a model of what today is called 'inculturation'—the incarnation of the Gospel in native cultures—and also the introduction of these cultures into the life of the Church" (21.1).

In doing this, Cyril and Methodius exhibited the wisdom of the householder in Jesus' parable who brings out of his storehouse both the new and the old (Mt. 13:52): "they always succeeded in maintaining perfect orthodoxy and consistent attention both to the deposit of tradition and to the new elements in the lives of the peoples being evangelized...once having purified and enlightened them by Revelation" (10.1, 11.2).

These principles of missionary activity clearly enunciated by Vatican II, are guiding principles for missionary activity today. As Pope John Paul II concluded, "their sowing of the Gospel seed did not cease to bear fruit, and their pastoral attitude of concern to bring the revealed truth to new peoples while respecting their cultural originality remains a living model for the Church and for missionaries of all ages" (7.3).

THE CATHOLICITY OF THE CHURCH

This missionary openness to the riches of different cultures flows from the 'catholicity' or universality of the Church that Pope John Paul explores in Chapter V of *Slavorum Apostoli*. He begins this chapter by speaking of Vatican II's goal of promoting "the proclamation of the eternal message of salvation, peace, and mutual concord among [all] peoples and nations" (16.2). This call to spread the Gospel to all is based on the teaching of the "Dogmatic Constitution on the Church" (*Lumen Gentium*) that "all men are called to belong to the new People of God. Wherefore this people, while remaining one and only one, is to be spread throughout the whole world...so that the decree of God's will may be fulfilled." Consequently, the Church embraces all peoples and fosters and takes to herself "insofar as they are good, the ability, riches and customs of which the genius of each people expresses itself. Taking them to herself she purifies, strengthens and ennobles them" (*LG* 13).

Pope John Paul proposes St. Cyril and Methodius as ones who possessed this "catholic" concept of the Church of Jesus Christ as embracing all peoples, times and cultures, and who put this belief into practice. He quotes St. Cyril's response to those who criticized them for this *catholic* outlook:

> Do not all breathe the air in the same way? And you are not ashamed to decree only three languages (Hebrew, Greek and Latin), deciding that all other peoples and races should remain blind and deaf? (17.3)

Cyril goes on to cite the Scripture texts teaching that *all* nations and peoples are to praise the Lord (cf. Phil. 2:11; Ps. 66:4; 117:1).

Pope John Paul II points out that the catholicity of the Church is not merely a static or a historical phenomenon, but reaches out to affirm "every real human value" and seeks "to win for God each and every human person, in order to unite them with one another and with him in his truth and his love" (19.1). Through the work of Sts. Cyril and Methodius,

> the Slavs were able to feel that they, too, together with the other nations of the earth were descendants and heirs to the promise made by God to Abraham…And thanks to their awareness of their own Christian identity, the Slavs took their destined place in the Church. (20)

THE ECUMENICAL DIMENSION

Another aspect of Cyril and Methodius, which is so important for today, is how they represent the unity of the Church. They lived at a time before the division of the Churches of the East and West, and yet it would have been easier for the two brothers to act as representatives of one or the other tradition. They did not. Byzantine by birth and sent by the Eastern emperor and patriarch, they also sought the confirmation and approval of the Pope to bring the Gospel to another culture, the Slavs, in their own language and according to their customs:

> The fervent solicitude shown by both brothers and especially by Methodius by reason of his episcopal responsibility, to preserve unity of faith and love between the Churches of which they were members, namely, between the Church of Constantinople and the Church of Rome on the one hand, and Churches which arose in the lands of the Slavs on the other, was and will always remain their great merit. (14.2)

Pope John Paul II alludes to Vatican II's "Decree on Ecumenism" (*Unitatis Redintegratio*) regarding the present-day call for Christians to tirelessly seek the restoration of full communion and unity:

> It seems in no way anachronistic to see Saints Cyril and Methodius as the authentic precursors of ecumenism, inasmuch as they wished to eliminate effectively or to reduce any divisions, real or

only apparent, between the individual communities belonging to
the same Church. (14.1)

Thus Cyril and Methodius are excellent examples of the consistent effort
needed to preserve (or restore) unity in the Church, a theme that Pope John
Paul II continued to stress throughout his pontificate, culminating in his 1995
encyclical letter on Christian unity, *Ut Unum Sint*. In this encyclical he calls
them "the champions and also the patrons of the ecumenical endeavor of the
sister Churches of East and West" (27.1).

INTO THE NEW MILLENNIUM

Sts. Cyril and Methodius lived over a thousand years ago, but Pope John Paul
II sees their lives as very relevant to the needs and concerns of the world enter-
ing the third millennium after Christ. He says that they may rightly be called
"by the family of Slav peoples as the fathers of both their Christianity and their
culture" (25.1). They represent the Christian "roots" of Europe and European
culture, which in the 1980s and 1990s was a hotly debated issue in the formation of the European Union. Did Pope John Paul have this in mind when he
wrote this as an encyclical letter? I have no doubt. He writes:

> Their work is an outstanding contribution to the formation of the
> common Christian roots of Europe, roots which by their strength
> and vitality are one of the most solid points of reference, which
> no serious attempt to reconstruct in a new and relevant way the
> unity of the Continent can ignore. (25.2)

However, the relevance of Sts. Cyril and Methodius at this time in history
extends far beyond the European scene. As we have discussed, these saints
represent the quest for unity in a complex political and religious situation, as
existed in their time. Their love for the *whole* Church: of the East and the West
and the emerging cultures recently coming to faith in Christ, is an inspiration
and model for all Christians today. Their missionary zeal with the approach of
"inculturation" shows the way we should be carrying out our task of evangelization, of Christian witness. They also were men who sought reconciliation
and a peaceful resolution of differences, working respectfully with proper authorities. As Pope John Paul comments:

Being Christian in our day means being builders of communion in the Church and in society. This calls for openness to others, mutual understanding, and readiness to cooperate through the generous exchange of cultural and spiritual resources. (27.2)

Fittingly, Pope John Paul II's concluding section of this encyclical letter is largely an extended prayer to the Father for peace, for unity, for Europe, for the spread of the Gospel and for the future of the world: that it will grow to become a *civilization of love* through the example and intercession of these two great saints.

QUESTIONS FOR REFLECTION

1. Reflect on the gifts and graces given to SS. Cyril and Methodius, and how these uniquely prepared them for their missionary work together.

2. Pope John Paul II calls SS. Cyril and Methodius "true models...[of those who] have accepted St. Paul's invitation to become all things to all people in order to redeem all" (*SA* 11.2). Consider how they did this.

3. SS. Cyril and Methodius were respectful and solicitous to the authority of the Pope in Rome and the Patriarch in Constantinople. Reflect on the continued relevance of their love for and commitment to the whole Church.

FOR FURTHER READING

- Pope John Paul II, That They May Be One...(*Ut Unum Sint*)
- Pope John Paul II, The Light of the East (*Orientale Lumen*)
- Vatican II, Decree on Eastern Catholic Churches (*Orientalium Ecclesiarum*)
- *Catechism*, 830–856 (The Church is Catholic)
- *Light for Life*, (God with Us Publications, Pittsburgh, PA) an Overview of the Faith for Byzantine Catholics in three parts: Part I, *The Mystery Believed*; Part 2, *The Mystery Celebrated*; Part 3, *The Mystery Lived*

5

Dominum et Vivificantem
"Lord and Giver of Life"

The Fifth Encyclical Letter of Pope John Paul II

May 18, 1986

Pope John Paul II's fifth encyclical letter, *Dominum et Vivificantem*, completes the Trinitarian teaching that began with his first encyclical letter on Christ, The Redeemer of Man (*Redemptor Hominis*), and continued with his second encyclical, which focused on the Father who is "rich in mercy" (*Dives in Misericordia*). Six years and two encyclical letters later, the Holy Father completed this triptych. He waited to publish it on the sixteenth century anniversary of the First Council of Constantinople (AD 381), when the Church formally defined the divinity of the Holy Spirit.

PURPOSE OF THE ENCYCLICAL

Rather than presenting a complete summary of the doctrine of the Holy Spirit, the encyclical invites us "to draw near to the Holy Spirit as the giver of life…the supreme source of [the Church's] unity…[and] the source and dynamic power of the Church's renewal" (2.2–3). It is a response to the call of Vatican II and Pope Paul VI to pursue a new study of and a new devotion to the Holy Spirit.

There is no detailed discussion of the procession of the Holy Spirit within the Trinity, no analysis of the *filioque* clause (the Latin phrase for the procession of the Holy Spirit from the Father "and the Son"—*filioque*), nor even mention of the "charisms" of the Holy Spirit in the Church that were given renewed emphasis at Vatican II (cf. *LG* 12). Instead, Pope John Paul II focused on the *saving* and *life-giving* mission of the Holy Spirit in the Church and in the world. These themes were developed in the encyclical's three parts, which we will examine now.

THE SPIRIT OF THE FATHER AND THE SON GIVEN TO THE CHURCH

The encyclical's first part introduces the Holy Spirit as the Paraclete ("counselor," "intercessor" or "advocate") and the Spirit of Truth. These personal titles are unique to the Gospel of St. John, which provides the framework for this first section. The Holy Spirit is the Church's counselor and teacher who witnesses to Jesus and who enabled the Apostles and now us, his followers, to witness to Jesus.

Pope John Paul focuses on the union between the Holy Spirit and Jesus, the Messiah, "the one who comes in the Holy Spirit, the one who possesses the fullness of this Spirit in himself and at the same time for others" (16.7). Jesus' entire messianic ministry is carried out in the Holy Spirit (cf. 20). He is led by the Spirit (cf. Lk. 4:1), prays and rejoices in the Holy Spirit (cf. Lk. 10:21; Mt. 11:25 f.), but most of all desires to give the Holy Spirit to all of humanity: "He will baptize you with the Holy Spirit" (Mt. 3:11; Lk. 3:16) (cf. 20, 22). John's Gospel emphasizes that Jesus cannot send the Spirit until he himself is "glorified" on the Cross and returns to the Father (24; cf. Jn. 16:7). When that was accomplished, the Spirit was sent as God's greatest gift ("Person-gift" in nos. 22, 23), to carry out Christ's work of Redemption in human hearts and minds (cf. 24), and thus "brings to fulfillment the new era of the history of salvation" (22.2).

The day of Pentecost is the "birth of the Church." Pope John Paul explains the relationship between the Johannine account of Jesus "breathing" the Spirit into the Apostles on Easter Sunday night and the Lukan account of Pentecost:

> This event [Pentecost] constitutes the definitive manifestation of what had already been accomplished in the same Upper Room on Easter Sunday...What had then taken place inside the Upper Room, "the doors being shut," later, on the day of Pentecost, is manifested also outside, in public. (25.2)

He then quotes Vatican II:

> Doubtless, the Holy Spirit was already at work in the world be-
> fore Christ was glorified. Yet on the day of Pentecost, he came
> down upon the disciples to remain with them forever. On that
> day the Church was publicly revealed to the multitude, and the
> Gospel began to spread among the nations by means of preach-
> ing. (25.3; cf. *Ad Gentes* 4)

Two catechetical points may be noted here. First, Pentecost is the time of the
birth of the Church because the Church emerges publicly and begins its mission, empowered by the Holy Spirit. Human birth refers to the time when the
baby comes "out of the womb and into the world." At Pentecost the Church
was born as the Holy Spirit came upon Jesus' disciples and drove them out
of the "womb" of the Upper Room (where they were awaiting his coming)
and into the world, to carry out the mission Christ had given them in power
(cf. Mt. 28:19, 20). Secondly, often I am asked why Pentecost is so important
because the Holy Spirit was sent in the Old Testament and (apparently) upon
Jesus' disciples when he sent them out to preach and to heal. The answer lies
in the quote above, "Yet on the day of Pentecost, he came down upon the
disciples to *remain* with them forever." Because of original sin the Holy Spirit
could not remain or "abide" in people, making them "temples of the Holy
Spirit." Only as a result of Christ's redeeming death, which atoned for original
sin and all subsequent sins, could the Holy Spirit be sent to remain or dwell
in the souls of the redeemed. This explains Jesus' insistence in John's Gospel
that the Holy Spirit could not be sent (to dwell in them and in the Church)
unless he were 'glorified' on the Cross. It is through Baptism, as the encyclical goes on to explain, that the Holy Spirit now comes to dwell in the souls of
the faithful. Further, the Spirit is sent to continue the mission and ministry of
the apostles through the Sacrament of Orders, and "through the Sacrament of
Confirmation [to] ensure that all who are reborn of water and the Holy Spirit
are strengthened by this gift. And thus, in a certain way, the grace of Pentecost
is perpetuated in the Church" (25.4).

In addition to the Holy Spirit working in the Church through the sacraments, "He both equips and directs her with hierarchical and charismatic
gifts and adorns with His fruits of his grace (cf. Eph. 4:11–12; 1 Cor. 12:4;
Gal. 5:22)" (*LG* 4). John Paul II indicates that the Second Vatican Council
provided a more complete pneumatology: indeed that the Council's teaching

is "essentially 'pneumatological'; it is permeated by the truth about the Holy Spirit," containing "precisely all that 'the Spirit says to the Churches' with regard to the present phase of the history of salvation," and "has made the Spirit newly 'present' in our difficult age" (*DetV* 26.1, 2).

The Holy Spirit remains with the Church and continues to guide her, especially in this age through the Second Vatican Council. The Holy Father ends the first part of his encyclical with a fervent admonition for the Church to implement the Second Vatican Council—"its teaching and its pastoral and ecumenical thrust"—while taking care to test or discern the true meaning and proper implementation of the Council, which "is especially necessary" because "the Council opened itself widely to the contemporary world" (26.2). The mission of the Church continues in the world through the guidance and power of the Holy Spirit who "with a marvelous providence directs the unfolding of time and renews the face of the earth" (26.2; *GS* 26).

THE SPIRIT WHO CONVINCES THE WORLD OF SIN

The "centerpiece" of *Dominum et Vivificantem* is an extended pastoral reflection on the mission of the Holy Spirit regarding sin. The key text is John 16:8: "And when he comes, he will convince the world concerning sin and righteousness and judgment" (27.1). The "judgment" is particularly reserved for Satan, since the mission of Christ is to save the human race from sin (cf. Jn. 3:17; 12:47) and thus to *remove* man from judgment (i.e. damnation; 27.4). Once again, John Paul II turns to the analysis of Vatican II's Pastoral Constitution *Gaudium et Spes* to describe the situation of humans (Christian anthropology) and the world, and to analyze the work of the Holy Spirit to "convince" people of sin through conscience.

The Holy Spirit is a "double gift" (31.2), and both aspects of the gift are essential. First, the Spirit of truth who "searches even the depths of God" (1 Cor. 2:10) reveals the truth of the reality and horror of sin, which is revealed in the Cross of Christ. The freely accepted suffering of the Son of God, the innocent One, reveals both the evil of sin and God's response to it. Yet Pope John Paul stresses that people cannot truly be "convinced" of the reality and horror of sin except by the Holy Spirit. Only the Spirit can effect a conversion of heart, which begins with conviction of sin, but is completed by the second part of the "double gift:...the gift of the certainty of redemption" (31.2).

The Holy Spirit not only convicts us of our sin, which would crush us and leave us without hope. The Spirit also gives us the hope of redemption and the power to overcome sin.

> "The gift of the Spirit" ultimately means a call to friendship...The Second Vatican Council teaches: "The invisible God out of the abundance of his love speaks to men as friends and lives among them, so that he may invite them and take them into fellowship with himself" [DV 2]. (34)

The Holy Spirit is the divine Love by which we have friendship and communion (fellowship) with God. As the encyclical explains:

> Whereas sin, by rejecting love, has caused the "suffering" of man which in some way has affected the whole of creation, the Holy Spirit will enter into human and cosmic suffering with a new outpouring of love, which will redeem the world. (39.3)

The Holy Spirit is both the love of God poured into human hearts (Rom. 5:5) and the "light" of consciences by which "he makes man realize his own evil and at the same time directs him towards what is good...Thus the conversion of the human heart, which is an indispensable condition for the forgiveness of sins, is brought about by the influence of the Counselor" (42.2, 3).

The Holy Father devotes three articles (43–46) to a profound exposition of the way the Holy Spirit works through the conscience, as explained in *Gaudium et Spes* (6), to convert the human "heart." And yet, he acknowledges that one of the greatest evils of our age is "the loss of the sense of sin" which Pius XII had declared was the greatest "sin" of the past century (47.1). This "hardness of heart" (to use the biblical term) opens people to the possibility of committing the sin of blasphemy against the Holy Spirit (Mt. 12:31 f; Mk. 3:28 f; Lk. 12:10). Those who refuse to acknowledge their sin (i.e. who refuse to repent and to be converted) cannot receive the forgiveness of their sin—they put themselves beyond the pale of God's mercy. "The blasphemy against the Holy Spirit consists precisely in the radical refusal to accept this forgiveness... the radical refusal to be converted" (46.7).

Actually, then, the sin against the Holy Spirit, "committed by the person who claims to have a 'right' to persist in evil—in any sin at all" (46.7) is not an uncommon sin today. Hence, Pope John Paul concludes this section with a fervent plea for the Church to pray that this sin will decrease in the world and instead that there will be a greater "openness of conscience necessary for the saving action of the Holy Spirit" and "a holy readiness to accept his mission as the Counselor, when he comes to 'convince the world concerning sin, and righteousness and judgment'" (47.2).

THE SPIRIT WHO GIVES LIFE

> The Church's mind and heart turn to the Holy Spirit as this twentieth century draws to a close and the third Millennium since the coming of Jesus Christ into the world approaches. (49.1)

These opening words of Part III of *Dominum et Vivificantem* speak volumes about Pope John Paul II. Sixteen years before the year 2000, he was anticipating the Great Jubilee and telling us, "the Church cannot prepare for the Jubilee in any other way than in the Holy Spirit" (51.1). Why? The Holy Father explains that the climax of human history, the "fullness of time," was the moment of the Incarnation in which God's self-communication, his gift of himself to humanity, reached its apex. This was accomplished through the Holy Spirit:

> The conception and birth of Jesus Christ are in fact the greatest work accomplished by the Holy Spirit in the history of creation and salvation: the supreme grace, "the grace of union," source of every other grace, as St. Thomas explains. (50.2)

Thus, the great Jubilee, celebrating the two thousandth anniversary of Christ's birth "has a pneumatological aspect," since the Holy Spirit was the author of this work (50.1).

Pope John Paul II realized that what was accomplished by Mary's faith two thousand years ago ("And faith…is the *openness* of the human heart to the gift: to *God's self-communication in the Holy Spirit*" [51.1; emphasis mine]) can only be renewed in our day by the same faith and openness to the Holy Spirit. The Spirit is the one "who gives life," and is the source of that divine life, by which we are reborn as sons and daughters of God and by which we cry "Abba, Father" (Rom. 8:15). Through the "uncreated gift" of the Spirit: "human life becomes permeated, through participation, by the divine life, and itself acquires a divine, supernatural dimension" (52.3).

The Holy Spirit has been the source of life of God's people for two thousand years. However, Pope John Paul II says that to celebrate the Jubilee, "We need to go further back, to embrace the whole of the action of the Holy Spirit even before Christ—from the beginning, throughout the world, and especially in the economy of the Old Covenant" (53.3). The Second Vatican Council "reminds us of the Holy Spirit's activity also 'outside the visible body of the Church'" and states that the Spirit offers to *every* person the possibility of salvation (53.3). The life of God extends in a mysterious way to all by the Holy Spirit: "he, the 'hidden God,' who as love and gift 'fills the universe'" (54.2).

THE LIFE GIVING SPIRIT OVERCOMES
THE "FLESH" AND THE "WORLD"

As *Dominum et Vivificantem* draws to a close, Pope John Paul discusses how the Holy Spirit, "who is the source of all God's salvific activity in the world" (54.2), "meets with resistance and opposition" (55.1). In the individual, the struggle is put in St. Paul's terms (in Gal. 5) of the "flesh" warring against the Spirit. Those who "walk" by the Spirit overcome the sins of the flesh and manifest "the fruit of the Spirit: love, joy, peace, patience, kindness, goodness, faithfulness, gentleness, self-control" (55.3, Gal. 5:22 f). The Holy Father assures us that in this struggle the victor will be "the one who welcomes the gift [of the Spirit]" (55.5).

However, the opposition to the Holy Spirit also is embodied in philosophical systems and ideologies that have become powerful forces in today's world: materialism, systematic atheism, and "signs of death" such as the arms race, "death-dealing poverty and famine," abortion and euthanasia (cf. 56, 57). Nonetheless, the Spirit who raised Christ from the dead, the "Lord and Giver of Life" comes to strengthen the "inner, spiritual person," and continues to communicate a new life that is stronger than death. The Holy Spirit, who "as [God's] gift to man, transforms the human world from within" (59.2), enables Christ's followers to give themselves through "a sincere gift of self" (*GS* 24) to God and others. By this means individuals and human communities discover true freedom, "the freedom of the Holy Spirit" (cf. 2 Cor. 3:17), freedom both from the "flesh" and "from the old and new determinisms," which attempt to control the modern world.

How do we receive this freeing and strengthening gift of the Spirit? Especially through the Church and her sacraments, in particular the Eucharist, Pope John Paul says. The Church is the "visible dispenser" of the life-giving signs we call "sacraments," "while the Holy Spirit acts in them as the *invisible dispenser* of the life which they signify" (63.3).

Finally, John Paul II calls the Church to prayer.

> The breath of the divine life, the Holy Spirit…expresses itself and makes itself felt in prayer…wherever people are praying in the world, there the Holy Spirit is, the living breath of prayer…Our difficult age has a special need of prayer. (65.1, 3)

Pope John Paul saw it as a "significant and comforting sign" that an increasing number of movements and groups "are giving first place to prayer and seeking in prayer a renewal of their spiritual life" (65.3). This is clearly a sign of the Holy Spirit's action, and is a source of Christian hope—even "the eschatological hope" that the fullness of God's Kingdom will be realized. "The Holy Spirit, given to the Apostles as the Counselor, is the guardian and animator of this hope in the heart of the Church" (66.3). The prayer of the faithful at the end of the Book of Revelation is to be our prayer today as we go forth boldly in the hope and power of the Holy Spirit into the third millennium: "The Spirit and the bride say to the Lord Jesus Christ: Come!" (66.3; Rev. 22:17).

QUESTIONS FOR REFLECTION

1. How was Jesus' entire ministry carried out in the Holy Spirit and how was his work continued, through the Holy Spirit, in the Church?

2. Pope John Paul II refers to the Holy Spirit as a "double gift" with regard to sin. What are these two aspects, and how are they experienced?

3. What is the relationship between conscience and the work of the Holy Spirit?

4. Why is prayer in and through the Holy Spirit indispensable for the life of the Church in every age?

5. What are sources of opposition to the work of the Holy Spirit in history?

6. Where can we look in the Church today to receive the life-giving Spirit?

FOR FURTHER READING

- Andrew Apostoli, CFR, *The Gift of God: The Holy Spirit*
- Raniero Cantalamessa, OFM Cap., *Come, Creator Spirit: Meditations on the Veni Creator*
- Raniero Cantalamessa, OFM Cap., *Sober Intoxication of the Spirit: Filled With the Fullness of God*
- Bede Jarrett, O.P., *Little Book of the Holy Spirit*
- Alan Schreck, *Your Life in the Holy Spirit*
- Frank Sheed, *The Action of the Holy Spirit*
- *Catechism*, Part 1, Section 2, Chapter 3, Article 8 (I Believe in the Holy Spirit, no. 687–747)
- *USCCA*, Chapter 9 (Receive the Holy Spirit)

6

Redemptoris Mater
"Mother of the Redeemer"

The Sixth Encyclical Letter of Pope John Paul II

March 25, 1987

John Paul II's special love for Mary is well known and is expressed succinctly and beautifully in his motto: *Totus Tuus* (totally yours). Every official document and address of John Paul II ends either with a reflection on Mary or a prayer for her intercession. One of his last major documents, *Rosarium Virginis Mariae* (on the Rosary in 2002), introduces the "Mysteries of Light" or Luminous Mysteries of the Rosary (no. 21), which celebrate the mysteries of Jesus' public ministry, culminating in his institution of the Eucharist.

It is not surprising, therefore, that Pope John Paul II, after he had written encyclical letters focusing on God the Father (*Dives in Misericordia*), the Son (*Redemptor Hominis*) and the Holy Spirit (*Dominum et Vivificantem*), turns his attention to Mary, the Mother of God and the first-born of humanity redeemed in Jesus Christ. He does this in this his sixth encyclical.

God entered into human history in the fullness of time "born of a woman" (Gal. 4:4)—Mary of Nazareth. John Paul explains that he is moved to reflect on Mary at the approach of the celebration of the two thousandth anniversary of the birth of Christ, and announces a "Marian year" from June 7 (Pentecost), 1988 through 1989 to celebrate Mary's birth (cf. 3), and "to promote a new and more careful reading of what the [Second Vatican] Council said about the Blessed Virgin Mary" (48.3). Thus this encyclical is part of what the Holy Father called a "new advent"—a time of preparation and reflection anticipating the coming of Christ in a new way at the Great Jubilee of the year 2000. Yet, what is presented in this letter is significant for Christians of all time, as it presents some of the central mysteries of our faith that are revealed in the person of Mary.

MARY IN THE MYSTERY OF CHRIST

Part I of *Redemptoris Mater* follows the pattern of the final chapter of Vatican II's "Dogmatic Constitution on the Church" (*Lumen Gentium*) in reflecting on the biblical teaching on Mary. It praises God, "who has blessed us in Christ with every spiritual blessing (Eph. 1:3)" (7.1). These blessing are seen in Mary, who like all the elect, was chosen in Christ, "before the foundation of the world [to] be holy and blameless before him" (Eph 1:4). In this plan of mercy and salvation, God "reserves a special place for the 'woman'"—Mary (7.2). The Father chose her alone to be the mother of his divine Son, and so at the Annunciation she is called "full of grace" by the angel Gabriel (Lk. 1:28) and later declared "blessed among women" under the inspiration of the Holy Spirit by her cousin Elizabeth at the Visitation (Lk. 1:42).

The central theme of John Paul II's reflection on Mary is her *faith*, highlighted in the words of Elizabeth: "'Blessed is she who believed that there would be a fulfillment of what was spoken to her from the Lord' (Lk. 1:45)" (12.3). Mary's response to God's revelation of his plan for her was to entrust her whole being to God through "the obedience of faith," a phrase in Vatican II's "Dogmatic Constitution on Divine Revelation" (*Dei Verbum*) that describes how *all* Christians are to respond to God's call and revelation. Mary's faith and openness to the action of the Holy Spirit was "perfect" (13.2), and "can also be compared to that of Abraham...[whose] faith constitutes the beginning of the Old Covenant; Mary's faith at the Annunciation inaugurates the New Covenant" (14.1).

Mary's faith, like Abraham's, was tested. The Annunciation—her "fiat" or "yes" to God's plan—enabled God to become incarnate "but it is also the point of departure from which her whole 'journey towards God' begins, her whole pilgrimage of faith" (14.2). Mary must also accept in faith the troubling words of Simeon that her son would be "a sign that is spoken against" (Lk. 2:34) and that "a sword will pierce through your own soul also" (cf. Lk. 2:34–35), a prophecy of Jesus' rejection by his own people and of Mary's unique sharing in her Son's Passion and death (cf. 16.2). Mary's sharing in the life and mystery of her Son through faith is largely a hidden one during his public ministry ("hid with Christ in God," cf. Col. 3:3), filled both with joy and sometimes with "a particular heaviness of heart, linked with a sort of 'night of faith'—to use the words of St. John of the Cross" (17.3). The depth and quality of Mary's faith is fully revealed at Calvary. "At the foot of the Cross Mary shares through faith in the shocking mystery of this self-emptying. This is perhaps the deepest 'kenosis' of faith in human history" (18.3). Pope John Paul notes, "in contrast with the faith of the disciples who fled, hers was far more enlightened" (Ibid). Mary had pondered the prophetic words of Simeon, and so understood the rejection of her son and her sharing in his suffering. Thus, from the Cross Jesus was able to look down upon her there and say to the beloved disciple "Behold your mother" (Jn. 19:27).

THE MOTHER OF GOD
AT THE CENTER OF THE PILGRIM CHURCH

"The words uttered by Jesus from the Cross signify that the motherhood of her who bore Christ finds a 'new' continuation in the Church and through the Church, symbolized and represented by John" (24.2). Pope John Paul II observes that the essential link between the birth of Christ and the birth of Church is Mary. "In both cases her discreet yet essential presence indicates the path of 'birth from the Holy Spirit'" (24.4). The second part of *Redemptoris Mater* focuses on Mary's presence in and through the "pilgrim Church," beginning with its birth in the Upper Room in Jerusalem on the day of Pentecost (cf. 25–26).

Like Mary, the Church too, is on a "pilgrimage of faith" through the power of the Risen Lord and of the Holy Spirit—a theme emphasized by the Second Vatican Council (25, cf. *LG* 9). Pope John Paul observes that Mary's "journey of faith" was *longer* than anyone else in that Upper Room, since she had begun following Christ from the Annunciation, and hence "Mary 'goes before them,' 'leads the way' for them" (26.2). Because she knew Jesus all of his life, both as his mother and as a faithful disciple, the Church honored her ("looked at Mary through Jesus") and also sought her witness to understand Jesus ("looked at Jesus through Mary") since "she was the first to believe" (26.5). Even though Mary was not sent out as an apostle to witness to Christ to the nations "this heroic faith of hers 'precedes' the apostolic witness of the

Church, and ever remains in the Church's heart" (27.1). John Paul II continually repeats the words of Elizabeth as a refrain throughout the document:

> Elizabeth's words, "Blessed is she who believed" continue to accompany the Virgin also at Pentecost; they accompany her from age to age, wherever knowledge of Christ's salvific mystery spreads…Thus is fulfilled the prophecy of the Magnificat: "All generations will call me blessed …" (Lk. 1:48–49). For knowledge of the mystery of Christ leads us to bless his Mother, in the form of special veneration for the Theotokos. (27.2)

The Pope stresses that Mary is especially to be honored and venerated *for her faith*—a faith that can strengthen and sustain ours in time of trial.

Christian unity is another theme of Part II of *Redemptoris Mater*. Mary has been a source of disunity among some Christians of the West, but this should not be so. John Paul II wrote that Mary reminds us of the truth that Christians are in communion with each other in the Holy Spirit and that "in this union the mystery of Pentecost is continually being accomplished" (28.2). Since Mary was the first to believe in Jesus and is, indeed, the model of faith, the Holy Father asks, "Why should we not all together look to her as *our common Mother*, who prays for the unity of God's family and who 'precedes' us all at the head of the long line of witnesses of faith in the one Lord, the Son of God, who was conceived in her virginal womb by the power of the Holy Spirit?" (30.3; emphasis mine). Already the Orthodox Church and the Catholic Church "feel united by love and praise of the Theotokos" (31.1). The Holy Father devotes four articles of the encyclical letter recalling the rich history of devotion in the Eastern Orthodox churches to Mary, which join our own Catholic tradition in lifting up a great "Magnificat" with Mary in praise of God. Mary's *Magnificat* also reminds us of God's "love of preference for the poor and humble, that love which, celebrated in the *Magnificat*, is later expressed in the words and works of Jesus" (37.2).

MATERNAL MEDIATION

Part III of *Redemptoris Mater* returns to a reflection on "Mary's mediation," which "is intimately linked with her motherhood" (38.3). In Pope John Paul's reflection on the biblical testimony to Mary in Part I he recalls Mary's first act of mediation—at the wedding feast at Cana. As in the chapter on Mary in *Lumen Gentium* (chap. 8), the Pope explains how Mary's mediation is "a sharing in the one unique source that is the mediation of Christ himself" (Ibid), just as the unique priesthood of Christ is shared by his priestly people.

The key to Mary's special role of intercession or mediation comes from her total *submission* to Jesus, as the "handmaid of the Lord," by which, at the Annunciation, she accepts motherhood according to the Lord's will (which is not by man, but by the Holy Spirit). It appears that Pope John Paul wishes to clarify that Mary's role as Mediatrix is not a claim to her "power" over God, but rather is the result and fruit of her perfect *submission* to God and his will, and a sharing in the mediation of Christ, the "one mediator between God and men" (1 Tim. 2:5). Mary is "left by her Son as Mother in the midst of the infant Church...After her Son's departure, her motherhood remains in the Church as maternal mediation: interceding for all her children, the Mother cooperates in the saving work of her Son, the Redeemer of the world" (40.1). Mary's motherly mediation (her prayer for her children) did not cease when she was taken up into heaven (her Assumption) but continues and "contributes in a special way to the union of the pilgrim Church on earth with the eschatological and heavenly reality of the Communion of Saints" (41.1), which will continue until Christ's final coming to earth at the end of time.

Until then, the Church continues to honor Mary and to follow her example of obedience and submission to God and his word. As Pope John Paul II expresses so beautifully, the Church learns her own motherhood from Mary.

> Like Mary, who first believed by accepting the word of God...so too the Church becomes a mother when, accepting with fidelity the word of God, "by her preaching and by baptism she brings forth to a new and immortal life children who are conceived of the Holy Spirit and born of God." (43.1; cf. *LG* 64)

THE MARIAN DIMENSION OF EVERY CHRISTIAN'S LIFE

Toward the end of the encyclical, we see a reflection of Pope John Paul II's "personalism" when he speaks of the "unique and unrepeatable relationship between two people: between mother and child and between child and mother" (45.1). Mary's motherhood "in the order of grace" means that Christ's words to the apostle John at the foot of the Cross, "Behold your mother," is an entrustment of humanity and of every disciple of Christ to Mary's mother-hood. It is "a gift which Christ himself makes personally to every individual" (45.3). So, each Christian is invited to discover what this means—to reflect on the love God has for us in Jesus Christ, that he would give to each of us besides a human mother, a spiritual mother to guide us and to pray for us. John Paul notes,

> This Marian dimension of the Christian life takes on special im-portance in relation to women and their status. (46.2)

Though he doesn't develop this topic here (it is discussed fully in his apostolic exhortation *Mulieris Dignitatem*, On the Dignity and Vocation of Women, he does indicate that Mary, who is "the woman" and "the new Eve," is the key to understanding women in God's plan.

John Paul II also speaks of the "profound link" between Mary and the presence of Jesus in the Eucharist and concludes: "Mary guides the faithful to the Eucharist" (44.4). It is a perfect example of the dictum "To Jesus through Mary." As the Mother of the Church, Mary is linked to all of the major *myster-ies* of human life and of God's saving plan. Thanks be to God for Pope John Paul II's insight into this great gift of Mary!

—————————— QUESTIONS FOR REFLECTION ——————————

1. Reflect on the blessings seen in Mary.

2. What are some things we can learn from the two aspects of Mary's faith: her "obedience of faith" and her "pilgrimage of faith?"

3. Mary's faith becomes a gift to the Church. Reflect on her continuing role, and our response.

4. Reflect on Mary's motherhood as a source of both unity among Christians and powerful mediation.

5. What might a personal application of this gift of Mary's motherhood, "which Christ makes personally to every individual" (45.3), look like?

FOR FURTHER READING

* Mark Miravalle, *Introduction to Mary: The Heart of Marian Doctrine and Devotion*
* Mark Miravalle, *Meet Mary*
* George T. Montague, S.M., *Our Father, Our Mother: Mary and the Faces of God*
* Marie-Dominique Philippe, O.P., *Mary Mystery of Mercy*
* Bl. John Henry Newman, *The New Eve*
* Alan Schreck, *The Essential Catholic Catechism*, Chapter 11
* NCCB, *Behold Your Mother: Woman of Faith*
* *Catechism*, 148–149; 484–507; 721–726; 963–975

7

Sollicitudo Rei Socialis
"On Social Concerns"

The Seventh Encyclical Letter of Pope John Paul II

December 30, 1987

Pope John Paul II's social encyclical, *Sollicitudo Rei Socialis*, commemorates the twentieth anniversary of Pope Paul VI's *Populorum Progressio*, "On the Development of Peoples" (1967). Some catechists and religious educators find it particularly challenging to prepare an instruction on the social teaching of the Church. However, we should not be deterred, because as John Paul II explained, presenting the Church's social doctrine is an essential "part of the Church's evangelizing mission" (41.8), applying the word of God to the actual conditions and circumstances of our day.

A GRIM REPORT

Vatican II's *Gaudium et Spes* stands behind these encyclicals with its emphasis on the dignity of the human person, on societies existing to promote the true welfare of persons and on the Church's duty of constantly "scrutinizing the signs of the times and of interpreting them in the light of the Gospel" (*GS* 4).

In Chapter 3 of *Sollicitudo*, John Paul II reviews worldwide progress toward greater human development, and his report is grim. Hopes for development "appear very far from being realized" (12.1); in fact, the gap between rich and poor, such as "the so-called developed North and the developing South" (14.1), appear to be widening rather than decreasing. The Holy Father points to the lack of adequate housing (17.2–17.4), rising unemployment (18.2–18.4) and growing international debt (19.1–19.6) as indicators of this. The "existence of two opposing blocs, commonly known as the East and the West" (20.3) has not, overall, improved the situation and has generally made it worse through promoting the arms race and a new form of imperialism or "neo-colonialism."

A REVIEW OF SOCIETY
IN LIGHT OF THE CHURCH'S SOCIAL DOCTRINE

Pope John Paul states that both the "liberal capitalism" of the West and the "Marxist collectivism" of the East have concepts of the development of individuals and peoples that are "imperfect and in need of radical correction" (20.5–21.1). The West is prone to "selfish isolation" as it pursues a sort of "super-development" for its own wealthy members (23.5, 28.2), while the East "seems to ignore…its duty to cooperate in the task of alleviating human misery" (23.5). By *super-development*, John Paul means "the so-called civilization of 'consumption' or 'consumerism,' which involves so much 'throwing-away' and 'waste'" (28.2). However, John Paul II insists that "the Church's social doctrine is not a 'third way' between liberal capitalism and Marxist collectivism, nor even a possible alternative to other solutions less radically opposed to one another: rather, it constitutes a category of its own" (41.7).

Technical progress is of less value than justice, brotherhood and a more humane social environment.

While these are of importance and interest to the specialist, the average reader may find these parts of the encyclical "heavy going." Hence I will devote the remainder of this chapter to focusing on the aspect of *development* that is the special concern of the Church: the moral theology that underlies all of the Holy Father's teaching in this encyclical letter.

MORAL THEOLOGY OF DEVELOPMENT

Chapter IV of *Sollicitudo Rei Socialis*, Authentic Human Development, reminds us that true human development is based on what a human person is, rather than on what he has. As Vatican II's *Gaudium et Spes* teaches:

> A man is more precious for what he is than for what he has. (cf. Col. 1:15) Similarly, all that men do to obtain greater justice, wider brotherhood, a more humane disposition of social relationships has greater worth than technical advances. For these advances

can supply the material for human progress, but of themselves alone they can never actually bring it about. (*GS* 35)

Sollicitudo rejects the myth of Enlightenment thought that technological progress will necessarily bring about a better world and foster the development of all peoples. Experience has taught us otherwise.

Yes, "development has a necessary economic dimension, since it must supply the greatest possible number of the world's inhabitants with an availability of goods essential for them 'to be'" (28.8). Yet true development must also take into consideration the "social, cultural, and spiritual dimensions of the human being" (9.9).

As with much of Pope John Paul II's thought, he develops his views "beginning at the beginning"—with the Book of Genesis. Pope John Paul reminds us that all of creation is a gift from God. Humans have dominion over creation (cf. Gen. 1:25–28), *but always as stewards who are subject to the will of God.* God imposes limits upon man's use of creation (cf. 29.3). He notes that *today's* "development" is but a chapter of the story which began at creation, "a story which is constantly endangered…by infidelity to the Creator's will, and especially by the temptation to idolatry" (30.6)—of "money, ideology, class, technology" (37.3). John Paul II then recalls the parable of the talents (cf. Mt. 25:26–28), in which God expects us to "receive the gifts of God in order to make them fruitful, to 'sow' and 'reap.' If we do not, even what we have will be taken away from us" (30.7). He concludes that these harsh words of our Lord are spoken to remind us of our "duty, which is urgent for everyone today, to work together for the full development of others: development of the whole human being and of all people" (30.8; *PP* 42).

ROOTED IN PERSONALISM

This concept of development represents both the teaching of Vatican II and so much of John Paul's *personalism*. Development is not just a social program or ideology, but a responsibility of each person. He notes that it is part of the Church's teaching and most ancient practice "to relieve the misery of the suffering, both far and near, not only out of her 'abundance' but also out of her 'necessities'" (31.7)—even selling superfluous Church ornaments and costly furnishings to assist the poor in cases of need.

Authentic human development is known by its moral character, "based on the dignity of the person and on the proper identity of each community, beginning with the family and religious societies, then all the rest" (33.4). True development respects and defends the rights of each person and of all social groups. Ultimately, because the full truth about the person and society is found in the Gospel of Christ, John Paul II concludes, "true development must be based on the love of God and neighbor…This is the 'civilization of love' of which Paul VI often spoke" (33.8). True development also includes the proper use of all created things, recognizing that natural resources are limited, the global ecological balance must be preserved and pollution of the environment must be avoided or minimized. This, too, is part of the moral dimension of development (cf. 34.1–34.6).

LEARNING TO READ MODERN PROBLEMS THEOLOGICALLY

After explaining the moral character of development, Pope John Paul asserts that "the *obstacles* to development likewise have a moral character" (35.1; emphasis mine). The Christian realizes the real obstacles to authentic human development cannot be explained merely as "short sightedness," "mistaken political calculations" or "imprudent economic decisions" (36.1). Beneath these explanations are the reality of sin and the "structures of sin," such as the all-consuming desire for profit at any price, and the thirst for power (36.3, 37.1). Individuals, nations and blocs can fall victim to these sins. *Gaudium et Spes* taught that the struggles of the modern world are symptoms of the struggle within the heart of each person who "suffers from internal divisions, and from these flow so many and such great discords in society" (*GS* 10).

Pope John Paul uses this analysis of sin to point out "the true *nature* of the evil, which faces us with respect to the development of peoples: it is a question of moral evil, the fruit of many sins, which lead to 'structures of sin'" (37.4; emphasis mine).

> This conversion specifically entails a relationship to God…It is God, in "whose hands are the hearts of the powerful" and the hearts of all, who according to his own promise and by the power of his Spirit can transform "hearts of stone" into "hearts of flesh." (38.4; cf. Ezek. 36:26)

SOLIDARITY

While so many of the "signs of the times" of which the encyclical speaks are discouraging and negative, at this point Pope John Paul II speaks of a positive sign of hope: "the growing awareness of interdependence among individuals and nations" (38.5). This is a sign of God's Spirit at work to instill in human hearts the virtue that is essential to achieving true development: *solidarity.* Solidarity is not a feeling, a program, or an attitude, but

> a firm and persevering determination to commit oneself to the common good; that is to say to the good of all and of each individual...[it is] a commitment to the good of one's neighbor with the readiness, in the Gospel sense, to "lose oneself" for the sake of the other instead of exploiting him, and to "serve him" instead of oppressing him for one's own advantage (cf. Mt. 10:40–42; 20:25; Mk. 10:42–45; Lk. 22:25–27). (38.6)

In this, I believe that John Paul II is only being realistic. Only with conversion of hearts that results in a widespread determination and commitment to seek the good of others is it realistic to expect an authentic development of peoples. We see a hopeful sign in the growing awareness of interdependence, but John Paul II adds that "interdependence must be transformed into solidarity, based upon the principle that the goods of creation are meant for all" (39.3).

> Solidarity helps us to see the "other"—whether a person, people, or nation—not just as some kind of instrument, with a work capacity and physical strength to be exploited at low cost and then discarded when no longer useful, but as our "neighbor," a "helper" (cf. Gen. 2:18–20), to be made a sharer, on a par with ourselves, in the banquet of life to which all are equally invited by God...Thus the exploitation, oppression and annihilation of others are excluded. (39.5)

One especially notable expression of this solidarity is the *preferential option or love for the poor.* This is an option, or a special form of primacy in the exercise of Christian charity, to which the whole Tradition of the Church bears witness. (cf. 42.2)

CONCLUSION

Pope Pius XII's motto was "peace as the fruit of justice." Pope Paul VI declared in *Populorum Progressio* (no. 87) that "development means peace these days." Building on these, John Paul II stated in *Sollicitudo Rei Socialis* that solidarity is the path to peace and at the same time to development, or more simply: "*Opus solidaritatis pax*, peace as the fruit of solidarity" (39.8) As he explained:

> The goal of peace, so desired by everyone, will certainly be achieved through the putting into effect of social and international justice, but also through the practice of the virtues which favor togetherness, and which teach us to live in unity, so as to build unity, by giving and receiving, a new society and better world. (39.9)

Pope John Paul II calls on the mercy of God especially through the intercession of the Blessed Virgin Mary, that true solidarity leading to peace may be attained on earth as it is in heaven.

-------------------- QUESTIONS FOR REFLECTION --------------------

1. What are the contributions from *Gaudium et Spes* that form the foundation of Pope John Paul's social teaching?

2. While today there is no "East" and "West" delineated as in 1987, comment on the relevance of Pope John Paul's review of worldwide progress toward human development.

3. What did Pope John Paul mean by the "moral dimension" of development?

4. Pope John Paul presents solidarity as the virtue essential to achieving true development. Consider the various attributes of solidarity. Pray that solidarity may grow in your heart and in the Church through the grace of the Holy Spirit.

FOR FURTHER READING

- John Paul II, On Human Work (*Laborem Exercens*)
- Paul VI, On the Development of Peoples (*Populorum Progressio*)
- Vatican II, Pastoral Constitution on the Church in the Modern World (*Gaudium et Spes*)
- *Catechism*, 2402–2449; 1905–1942

8

Redemptoris Missio
"The Mission of the Redeemer"

The Eighth Encyclical Letter of Pope John Paul II

December 7, 1990

In his encyclical letter, *Redemptoris Missio*, Pope John Paul II perceives two contrary trends: on the one hand the appearance of a "new springtime" of Christianity marked by "a new awareness that *missionary activity is a matter for all Christians*" (2.1), in contrast to the fact that "missionary activity specifically directed 'to the nations' (*ad gentes*) appears to be waning," which is "a sign of a crisis of faith" (2.2).

Is the Catholic Church in the midst of a resurgence of missionary activity, or in missionary doldrums? This reflects the broader question of where the Church stands since the Vatican Council. Has the Council brought renewal? Do we see greater understanding of the mission of the Church, and renewed zeal among Catholics to carry it out? Whatever your response, Pope John Paul II's purpose in writing this encyclical letter is clearly and forcefully stated:

> I wish to invite the Church to *renew her missionary commitment*...
> For missionary activity renews the Church, revitalizes faith and
> Christian identity, and offers fresh enthusiasm and new incentive.
> *Faith is strengthened when it is given to others!* ...
>
> But what moves me even more strongly to proclaim the urgency
> of missionary evangelization is the fact that it is the primary ser-
> vice which the Church can render to every individual and to all

humanity in the modern world, a world which has experienced
marvelous achievements but which seems to have lost its sense
of ultimate realities and of existence itself. "Christ the Redeemer,"
I wrote in my first encyclical, "fully reveals man to himself...The
person who wishes to understand himself thoroughly...must...
draw near to Christ...[The] Redemption that took place through
the cross has definitively restored to man his dignity and given
back meaning to his life in the world." (2.3–4)

Even in the introduction to this encyclical the missionary fervor of John Paul II
shines forth clearly and powerfully. You have the sense that this man, just like
St. Paul or St. Francis Xavier, personally would convert the world to Christ, if
he could. He cries out, *Peoples everywhere, open the doors to Christ!* (3.1). To
the non-Christian, he appeals:

His Gospel in no way detracts from man's freedom, from the
respect that is owed to every culture and to whatever is good
in each religion. By accepting Christ, you open yourself to the
definitive Word of God, to the One in whom God has made
himself fully known and has shown us the path to himself. (3.1)

To the Christian, especially to the Catholic faithful, he exhorts:

God is opening before the Church the horizons of a humanity
more fully prepared for the sowing of the Gospel. I sense that
the moment has come to commit all of the Church's energies to
a new evangelization and to the mission *ad gentes*. No believer in
Christ, no institution of the Church can avoid this supreme duty:
to proclaim Christ to all peoples. (3.4)

JESUS CHRIST, THE ONLY SAVIOR

Tragically, Vatican II's teaching on religious liberty and the possibility of salvation of any person, Christian or non-Christian, opened the door to the error
(*never* stated nor implied by the Council) that Jesus and his Church are not
necessary for salvation and that other religions were equally valid or expedient
ways to God and eternal salvation.

Pope John Paul II decided to begin this encyclical letter on missionary activity with a strong, clear and convicting statement that Jesus alone is the world's savior. He "pulls no punches" in stating the questions:

> Is missionary work among non-Christians still relevant? Has it not been replaced by inter-religious dialogue? Is not human development an adequate goal of the Church's mission? Does not respect for conscience and for freedom exclude all efforts at conversion? (4.3)

The answer to these difficult questions is simple, direct, and biblical: "No one comes to the Father, but by me" (Jn. 14:6); "And there is salvation in no one else, for there is no other name under heaven given among men by which we must be saved" (Acts 4:12).

Pope John Paul II comments: "This statement, which was made to the Sanhedrin, has a universal value, since for all people—Jews and Gentiles alike—salvation can only come from Jesus Christ" (5.1).

Besides being the "definitive self-revelation of God," Jesus also brings a "*radical newness of life*" (7.1). Jesus enables human beings to discover the full reality and mystery of who they are, which cannot be reduced to the "horizontal dimension alone" (8.1). In order for every person to be fully human and fully alive with a "radical newness of life," they must come to know Jesus Christ and invite him into their lives.

THE KINGDOM OF GOD

In the second chapter of *Redemptoris Missio*, Pope John Paul II explores the nature of the Kingdom that Jesus proclaimed, and concludes that "the kingdom cannot be detached either from Christ or from the Church" (18.1). First, he explains, "The Kingdom of God is not a concept, a doctrine, or a program subject to free interpretation, but it is before all else *a person* with the face and name of Jesus of Nazareth" (18.2). Jesus *is* the Kingdom, and the Church is "at the service of the Kingdom" (20.1), making Jesus known and present. Thus, "the Church is the sacrament of salvation for all mankind…a dynamic force in mankind's journey toward the eschatological Kingdom [i.e. the Kingdom fulfilled in heaven], and is a sign and promoter of Gospel values [on earth]" (20.4). The Church also serves the Kingdom by *intercession*, recognizing that the Kingdom is God's gift and God's work.

THE HOLY SPIRIT: THE PRINCIPAL AGENT OF MISSION

"The Holy Spirit is indeed the principal agent of the whole of the Church's mission" (21.2). Pope John Paul II sees the work of the Holy Spirit as closely related to Jesus' "missionary mandate" to make disciples of all nations (Mt. 28:18–20). All of these "commission" texts at the end of the Gospels share two elements (23.1):

- the universality of the mission (the apostles are sent to *all* peoples)

- the assurance that Jesus will not leave them alone in this task, but he will be with them, and will send the Holy Spirit to empower them to carry out this task

Also, since "the ultimate purpose of mission is to enable people to share in the communion which exists between the Father and the Son" (23.3), it is the Holy Spirit himself who is the bond of love and union between the Father and Son, and who (therefore) draws others into this loving communion, which is the ultimate purpose of the Church's mission. The Holy Spirit not only empowers the missionary, but also is a guide, which is particularly important today in discerning how the Gospel can be embodied properly in the culture of various peoples (cf. 25.2–3).

Pope John Paul summarizes the Holy Spirit's missionary work as giving life to the Church, impelling her to proclaim Christ, implanting his gifts in all peoples, and guiding the Church "to discover these gifts, to foster them, and to receive them through dialogue" (29.3).

THE VAST HORIZON OF THE MISSION *AD GENTES*

In the opening chapters of *Redemptoris Missio*, Pope John Paul II demonstrated the way in which the Church's missionary activity, her proclamation of the Kingdom through the work of the Holy Spirit, flows naturally from her acknowledgement of Jesus Christ as Savior. The fourth chapter continues with a discussion of the particular needs of the modern world. Modern society "demands a *resurgence of the Church's missionary activity.* The horizons and possibilities for mission are growing ever wider, and we Christians are called to an apostolic courage based upon trust in the Spirit" (30.1).

In the religious picture of the world today, which is "extremely varied and ever changing" (32.1), Pope John Paul notes three distinct situations faced by the Church:

- areas where the message of Christ has not been heard (33.2)

- "Christian communities with adequate and solid ecclesial structures," which bear effective witness to the Gospel (33.3)

- places "where entire groups of the baptized have lost a living sense of the faith, or even no longer consider themselves members of the Church, and live a life far removed from Christ and his Gospel" (33. 4)

The Holy Father insists that the missionary task "to the nations" (*ad gentes*) has priority as "the first task of the Church" (34.2), and yet he also contends that "churches in traditionally Christian countries…cannot be missionaries to non-Christians in other countries and continents unless they are seriously concerned about the non-Christians at home" (34.3). Here I think he is speaking about nominal or "lapsed" Catholics in traditionally Christian/Catholic countries, who need "re-evangelization."

Rapid worldwide changes (demographic, political and economic) especially in nations of the southern hemisphere, call for special attention in terms of the Church's missionary activity. In many of these countries, the young comprise over half the population. The Church must consider how to proclaim Christ to non-Christian young people who are the future of entire continents (cf. 37.b).

Another new challenge to the Church's mission is the result of modern scientific and technological advances. The influence of mass media requires Catholics to consider how the Gospel of Christ should be proclaimed, not just by using the media, but also in the culture formed by the media, scientific research and international relations (cf. 37.c).

Fortunately, many people immersed in these cultures are seeking "the spiritual dimension of life…as an antidote to dehumanization" (38.1). It is the Church's mission and duty to reach out to all these people, respecting their religious freedom "especially in those [countries] with a Catholic majority." Pope John Paul insists that Catholics respect and promote religious freedom:

"*The Church proposes: she imposes nothing.*" Likewise, he appeals to governments who restrict religious freedom to "*Open the doors to Christ!*" (39.2).

PATHS OF MISSION

Missionary activity, by its very nature, "develops in a variety of ways" (41.2). Pope John Paul II highlights the ways that are of principal importance for the Church in the modern world.

Witness, "*the very life of the missionary, of the Christian family,* and *of the ecclesial community,* which reveal a new way of living" (42.2), is the primary form of evangelization. The witness that "the world finds most appealing is that of concern for people, and of charity toward the poor, the weak and those who suffer" as well as "a commitment to peace, justice, human rights and human promotion" (42.3).

However, all witness *must* include a *clear initial* proclamation that Jesus is the only savior for all people. This proclamation of Jesus "is to be made with an attitude of love and esteem toward those who hear it," recognizing that the Holy Spirit is already at work in them stirring up the desire to know the truth about God (cf. 44, 45).

The Holy Father says that the aim of this proclamation is "*Christian conversion*": faith, which leads to *baptism.* Here Pope John Paul II addresses directly the objection that Christians should not "proselytize," but should "help people to become more human or more faithful to their own religion" or should just "build communities working for justice, freedom, peace and solidarity." He responds: "What is overlooked is that every person has the right to hear the 'Good News' of the God who reveals and gives himself in Christ" (46.4).

The response of faith and baptism requires a local *Church*—either already in existence or to be established—where those converted to Christ can live out their Christian life and become a witness of Christ to others:

> Every church, even one made up of recent converts, is missionary by its very nature, and is both evangelized and evangelizing. Faith must always be presented as a gift of God to be lived out in community (families, parishes, associations), and to be extended to others through witness in word and deed. The evangelizing activity of the Christian community, first in its own locality, and

then elsewhere as part of the Church's universal mission, is the clearest sign of a mature faith. (49.2)

John Paul II acknowledges that the Church's witness to Christ must take into account the necessity and challenges of divided Christian bodies witnessing together: the ecumenical dimension. The modern ecumenical movement was initiated by those who experienced the obstacles to conversion to Christ caused by division among Christians in mission territories. "The fact that the Good News of reconciliation is preached by Christians who are divided among themselves weakens their witness. It is thus urgent to work for the unity of Christians" (50.1).

On the other hand, one of the most promising developments in mission lands is the formation of "ecclesial basic communities": groups of Christians who "come together for prayer, Scripture reading, catechesis…" (51.1). Pope John Paul calls these communities a sign of vitality in the Church, and seedbeds for "a new society based on a 'civilization of love'" (Ibid). Within those communities and through other means the integration of the Catholic faith with their human culture takes place: "*inculturation*." This is "a difficult process, for it must in no way compromise the distinctiveness and integrity of the Christian faith" (52.2), but it must be undertaken for peoples to embrace Christianity while retaining the authentic goods and true values ("traditions"), which is their human heritage.

The path to the evangelization of peoples of different cultural and religious heritages will often entail *dialogue*, by which these peoples and their cultural heritage are genuinely understood by the missionaries. Through dialogue, the Church "seeks to uncover the 'seeds of the Word,'…found in individuals and in the religious traditions of mankind" (56.1).

"Dialogue should be conducted…with the conviction that *the Church is the ordinary means of salvation* and that *she alone* possesses the fullness of the means of salvation" (55.3). "*Dialogue does not dispense from evangelization*" (55.1). However, all dialogue ought to be conducted in faith and love, bearing witness to Christ (cf. 57).

This dialogue may involve *awakening people's consciences* to the values of Christ and his Gospel. If Catholics wish to promote economic, technical or political development in developing nations, Pope John Paul II urges them not to forget that "authentic human development must be rooted in an ever deeper evangelization" which offers people through Christ the opportunity "not to 'have more' but to 'be more'" (58.2). He challenges us "to turn to a more austere way of life," rooted in the greatest witness—active charity, that shows that true development must be based on ethical and religious values and not merely on economic progress and an increase of wealth (cf. 59).

WHO CARRIES OUT MISSIONARY ACTIVITY?

While all are called to proclaim the Gospel of Christ, certain vocations entail particular missionary activities. As successors of St. Peter and the apostles of Jesus, the Pope and the bishops "are directly responsible...for the evangelization of the world" (63.2). Hence, they encourage missionary vocations and send out missionaries to the world, including bishops sending out priests from their own dioceses for missionary service. In the missions they will work with those in consecrated or religious life, and also with the laity, among whom "catechists have a place of honor...Catechists are specialists, direct witnesses, and irreplaceable evangelizers who, as I have often stated and experienced in my missionary journeys, represent the basic strength of Christian communities, especially in the young churches." (73.1, 2).

The Catholic Church's efforts are coordinated worldwide by specific Vatican congregations, such as the Congregation for the Oriental Churches, and (especially) the Congregation for the Evangelization of Peoples. Nonetheless, all Catholics are called to participate in the missionary work of the Church through prayer and sacrifice for missionaries, and other forms of support (including financial) for the missions and missionary societies (cf. 78–85).

MISSIONARY SPIRITUALITY

The final chapter of *Redemptoris Missio* focuses on the spirituality of the missionary, which might be summarized as "a life of complete docility to the Spirit...It is not possible to bear witness to Christ without reflecting his image, which is made alive in us by grace and the power of the Spirit" (87.2). The challenges of the mission of the Church today "demands the courage and light of the Spirit" which flows from "intimate communion with Christ" (cf. 87–88):

> The missionary is urged on by "zeal for souls"...The missionary
> is a person of charity...The missionary is the "universal brother,"
> bearing in himself the Church's spirit, her openness to and interest

in all peoples and individuals, especially the least and poorest of his brethren...Finally, like Christ he must love the Church [as Christ did (cf. Eph. 5:25)]. (89.2–4)

Pope John Paul knew that holiness is the key to the success of the missionary, and reminded us, "Every member of the faithful is called to holiness and to mission" (90.2).

He stressed that missionaries must "update their doctrinal and pastoral formation" (proper formation is essential), but most of all "the missionary must be a 'contemplative in action'...Unless the missionary is a contemplative he cannot proclaim Christ in a credible way" (91.2).

The last characteristic of the missionary not only perfectly expresses the central goal of all Catholic Christians but also beautifully captures the vision of this encyclical. The missionary must be a "person of the Beatitudes" who exhibits "the inner joy that comes from faith":

In a world tormented and oppressed by so many problems, a world tempted to pessimism, the one who proclaims the "Good News" must be a person who has found true hope in Christ. (91)

—————————— QUESTIONS FOR REFLECTION ——————————

1. What are three reasons Pope John Paul II invites the Church to renew her missionary commitment?

2. Why is missionary activity still primary in an age of inter-religious dialogue and human development?

3. In what ways is the Holy Spirit the principal agent of mission?

4. What are the three distinct situations facing the Church, related to her missionary endeavor, that Pope John Paul II notes?

5. Reflect on witness as the primary form of evangelism, its means, its content and its goal.

6. Compare "dialogue," "inculturation" and "witness" and their roles in missionary work.

FOR FURTHER READING

- Ralph Martin and Peter Williamson, eds., *Pope John Paul and the New Evangelization*
- Second Vatican Council, Decree on the Church's Missionary Activity (*Ad Gentes*)
- Pope Paul VI, On Evangelization in the Modern World (*Evangelium Nuntiandi*)
- *Catechism*, 839–845; 849–856; 904–907

9

Centesimus Annus
"On the Centenary of *Rerum Novarum*"

The Ninth Encyclical Letter of Pope John Paul II

May 1, 1991

Pope Leo XIII's encyclical, *Rerum Novarum* (May 15,1891), is recognized as the first "social encyclical" of modern times. It applies Christian principles to questions about the rights of laborers, which had emerged especially as a result of the "industrial revolution." In his introduction to *Centesimus Annus*, Pope John Paul II proposes to undertake a "rereading" of *Rerum Novarum*, examining the "worker question" at the end of the twentieth century. Though the idea of the Church "speaking out" on social issues is still controversial in some quarters, John Paul speaks "of many millions of people, who, spurred on by the social Magisterium, have sought to make that teaching the inspiration for their involvement in the world…These people represent *a great movement for the defense of the human person* and the safeguarding of human dignity" (*CA* 3.4).

THE NEW ECONOMIC SITUATION

Chapter I of *Centesimus Annus* describes the new economic situation that emerged in the nineteenth century and which gave rise to modern Catholic social teaching. There emerged "a new form of property" (capital) and "labor" (workers) that "became a commodity to be freely bought and sold on the market" (4.3), often without regard for the bare minimum needed for the support of a worker and his family. Unemployment could result in starvation, in the absence of any kind of social security.

In response, various political theories emerged such as "socialism" that often advocated violent revolution. It was in this context that Pope Leo XIII spoke out, enunciating principles that could lead to the resolution of "*the conflict between capital and labor*, or…the worker question" (5.2), in a just and peaceful way. Leo XIII viewed this proclamation of the Gospel in political, social and economic matters as an essential part of the Church's evangelizing mission. Pope John Paul states that it is also an essential element of the "new evangelization" today (cf. 5.6).

In this encyclical letter, the Holy Father highlights the present-day importance of *Rerum Novarum*'s teaching on political structures. All individual's rights must be safeguarded, especially those of the defenseless and poor, and the State must make provision to assist and support those citizens in great need. John Paul notes that these principles are very relevant today in a world in which poverty abounds. The principle of care for those in need, which he calls "solidarity," has been echoed in Leo XIII's concept of "friendship," Pius XI's view of "social charity" and Pope Paul VI's teaching on building a "civilization of love" (cf. 10.3). However, Leo XIII did not expect the State to solve every social problem: "he frequently insists on necessary limits to the State's intervention" (11.2). Rather, the "main thread" and the "guiding principle" of Leo XIII's social teaching and that of the whole Church "is a *correct view of the human person* and of his unique value" (11.3).

TOWARD THE "NEW THINGS" OF TODAY

In the second chapter of *Centesimus Annus*, John Paul II applies those principles of *Rerum Novarum* to today. He notes that what *Rerum Novarum* foresaw has proven to be "surprisingly accurate" (12.1), particularly the weaknesses of socialism that culminated in the "breakdown" of that system in 1989. "By defining the nature of the socialism of his day as the suppression of private property, Leo XIII arrived at the crux of the problem" (12.3). Pope John Paul saw that the fundamental error of socialism is anthropological: the person is just an element or 'cog' in the social organism, whose personal good is subordinated to the smooth functioning of the socialist State. All the other errors of socialism flow from this one.

"In contrast," the Holy Father argues, "from the Christian vision of the human person there necessarily follows a correct picture of society" (13.2). In the Christian view, between the individual and the State are also intermediate groups, such as the family, which must be respected. Other errors of social-ism foreseen by *Rerum Novarum* include atheism (13.3), class struggle "not restrained by ethical or juridical considerations, or by respect for the dig-nity of others" (14.2), and State control of the means of production, without private ownership (15.1).

THE TWENTIETH CENTURY: TRAGEDIES AND TRIUMPHS

Rerum Novarum's prophetic message, while welcomed by many, "was not fully accepted by people at the time," which led to "some very serious tragedies" in the twentieth century (16.3). The World Wars and other conflicts, the arms race, and terrorism promoted by extremist groups were dramatically opposed to the message of *Rerum Novarum*. After World War II, atheistic communist to-talitarianism vied with democratic regimes and free market economic systems, which created "the consumer society" (19.4). Ironically, while the free market society showed itself capable of achieving greater prosperity than Marxist so-cialism, "it agrees with Marxism, in the sense that it totally reduces man to the sphere economics and the satisfaction of material needs" (19.4).

For Pope John Paul II, the year 1989 was a landmark as the practice of non-violent resistance and protest led to the collapse of communist totalitar-ian regimes in Eastern Europe, including Poland. What caused this collapse? Pope John Paul II pointed to the violation of the rights of workers (23.1) and the insufficiency of the communist economic system (24.1). However, "the true cause . . . was the spiritual void brought about by atheism" (24.2). Writing this encyclical letter in the immediate aftermath of the collapse of communism in Europe, John Paul noted, "for some countries of Europe the real post-war period is just beginning" (28.1). Resources must be found for the needed re-construction, such as could "be made available by disarming the huge military machines which were constructed for the conflict between East and West" (28.3). Economic development is sorely needed in many countries, but John Paul II reminds us, "The apex of development is the exercise of the right and duty to seek God, to know him and to live in accordance with that knowledge" (29.1). The great risk in the world to come will be that spiritual development will be forgotten or take a "back seat" to utilitarian values, that old forms of totalitarianism will re-emerge, or new forms of religious fundamentalism will deny to some their full exercise of civil and religious liberties. John Paul II reminds us that, "No authentic progress is possible without respect for the natural and fundamental right to know the truth and live according to that truth…[This] includes the right to discover and freely to accept Jesus Christ, who is man's true good" (29.c).

THE QUESTION OF PRIVATE PROPERTY

The fourth chapter of *Centesimus Annus* summarizes the Church's position on a question addressed by Leo XIII: reconciling the "right" of private property ownership with the belief that the goods of the earth are to be shared among all people (the "universal destination of material goods"). The biblical principle behind this reflection is Genesis 1:28, where God gives the human race dominion over the earth. Human beings exercise this dominion through their work. "In this way, he makes part of the earth his own, precisely the part which he has acquired through work; this is the *origin of individual property*. Obviously, he also has the responsibility not to hinder others from having their own part of God's gift" (31.2).

Today, ownership is more than that of land: an even more valuable commodity is "*the possession of know-how, technology and skill*" (32.1). Indeed, this points to the truth that the greatest resource today is "*man himself*, that is, his knowledge," his ability to organize, and "his ability to perceive the needs of others and to satisfy them" (32.4).

Just as in the past people were marginalized and kept dependent because of their inability to own land or possess capital, today people may be marginalized and exploited if they do not have access to land, money, *and* knowledge or training to enable them to participate in the building and advancement of the societies in which they live. "In fact, for the poor, to the lack of material goods has been added a lack of knowledge and training which prevents them from escaping their state of humiliating subjection" (33.2).

> If the goal of the Christian is to provide all people an opportunity to share fairly in the goods of the world, then it is necessary to break down the barriers and monopolies which leave so many countries on the margins of development, and to provide all individuals and nations with the basic conditions which will enable them to share in development. This goal calls for programmed and responsible efforts on the part of the entire international

community. Stronger nations must offer weaker ones opportunities for taking their place in international life. (35.4)

The Holy Father suggested that one specific step toward the realization of this is to "lighten, defer or even cancel the debt" that developing nations have to affluent nations and corporations (35.5). In his 2001 letter, *Novo Millennio Ineunte*, Pope John Paul repeated this call for the cancellation of the debts of poor countries, as a concrete response of nations to the "great Jubilee" of the year 2000. The great obstacle to such generous actions is the increasing consumerism of developed nations, which impels them to want to possess more and grow ever wealthier. John Paul II says, "It is not wrong to want to live better; what is wrong is a style of life which is presumed to be better when it is directed toward 'having' rather then 'being,' and which wants to have more, not in order to be more but in order to spend life in enjoyment as an end in itself" (36.4). Pope John Paul wishes to promote the pursuit of truth, beauty, goodness and communion with others, which necessitates the fostering of a "human ecology" in which man enables himself and others to pursue fullness of life and to share that life with others. The family (founded on the marriage of a man and a woman) is "the first and fundamental structure for 'human ecology'" (39.1). The family is to be seen as *"the sanctuary of life"* (39.2) in which each person is welcomed and valued. Where economic life is absolutized, attitudes valuing things over people can easily arise. The Holy Father refers to the Marxist concept of "alienation": "A man is alienated if he refuses to transcend himself and to live the experience of self-giving and of the formation of an authentic human community oriented toward his final destiny, which is God" (41.3). A society is "alienated" if it is structured in such a way that it makes it difficult for its members to give themselves to others and to God.

What sort of political and economic system allows the Christian vision of reality, the true 'human ecology' to emerge and succeed? "The Marxist solution has failed, but the realities of marginalization and exploitation remain in the world" (42.3). What of "capitalism"? The Holy Father distinguishes between a capitalism that does reflect and promote the Christian idea of human freedom and self-giving (perhaps called more appropriately a "business economy," "market economy," or "free economy"), and a "capitalism" without ethical and religious norms that is not at the service of human freedom, but presumably is enslaved to a selfish consumerist mentality. Obviously this latter form of "capitalism" does not reflect or promote a Christian vision of reality (cf. 42.1–2). "The Church" says, Pope John Paul, "has no models to present" (43.1). Her task is to set forth the Christian principles and vision; it is the ongoing task of individuals and societies to embody these ideals by creating political, social and economic systems that respect the person and reflect true human values.

MAN, THE STATE AND THE SACRED ORDER

In the final two chapters of *Centesimus Annus*, Pope John Paul II presents the Catholic Church's views of the relationship between the human person, the State, and the various economic, political and social systems that are dominant in the world today. The title of the encyclical's last chapter, "Man is the Way of the Church," enunciates the basic principle behind the Church's social teaching. It can be summarized by the simple statement that the State and the social, political and economic orders exist for the good and the benefit of the individual person, and for the protection and promotion of the individual person's rights and dignity (cf. 53.1–2).

An example of this is what *Centesimus Annus* teaches about "the *role of the State in the economic sector*" (48.1). The State must insure that its citizens are secure "so that those who work and produce can enjoy the fruits of their labors and thus feel encouraged to work efficiently and honestly" (Ibid). The State also directs the exercise of human rights in the economic sector, stimulates business opportunities and yet must avoid the danger of becoming a "Welfare State" (48.4). The State should promote the role of the family and other vital communities of persons by observing the principle of subsidiarity and promoting solidarity and charity among all those groups, which comprise the very fabric of a society. In all these ways, the true good of individual persons is promoted.

The Church's social teaching is a part of the "good news" that Jesus Christ came to live and proclaim. At the heart of God's law that Jesus accentuated, is *love*. *Centesimus Annus* explains that: "Love for others, and in the first place, love for the poor, in whom the Church sees Christ himself, is made concrete in the *promotion of justice*" (58). Justice is giving each person his or her due, and hence the administration and promotion of justice, whether personally or at the national or international level, is really all about promoting the good of (and loving) each individual person, whom God created in his image and likeness and for whom Christ died.

The encyclical's penultimate chapter addresses the Church's view of the State and the various political, social and economic systems that States employ. The basic principle in this chapter is that every legitimate system must acknowledge and found itself upon objective and transcendent truth. "If one does not acknowledge transcendent truth, then the force of power takes over" (44.2). Of course, one of these truths is "the transcendent dignity of the human person." "The root of modern totalitarianism" is found in the denial of this essential truth: that individual persons have God-given inviolable rights and dignity.

If the Church favors any political system, it is democracy, "inasmuch as it ensures the participation of citizens in making political choices, guarantees to the governed the possibility both of electing and holding accountable those who govern them, and of replacing them through peaceful means when appropriate" (46.1). However, the Holy Father rejects a current view that true democracy must correspond to a philosophy of agnosticism and skeptical relativism, since in a democracy no one can "impose" absolute beliefs or values on others. Pope John Paul points out, "if there is no ultimate truth to guide and direct political activity, then ideas and convictions can easily be manipulated for reasons of power. As history demonstrates, a democracy without values easily turns into open or thinly disguised totalitarianism" (46.2).

The Church also rejects a "fanaticism or fundamentalism" that "claim the right to impose on others their own concept of what is true and good. *Christian truth* is not of this kind" (46.3). Christians seek, not to impose their values or beliefs on others, but (respecting the transcendent dignity of the person) to propose what we believe to be true, knowing that "freedom attains its full development only by accepting the truth" (46.4).

Many of these truths that the Church proposes Christians consider foundational and essential for the life of society. Concern for the promotion and protection of human rights is one of these essential values that Christians believe must form the basis of a just society. *Centesimus Annus* lists some of these fundamental rights in article 47.

The Holy Father grieves that "even in countries with democratic forms of government, these rights are not always fully respected"; and that these democracies "seem at times to have lost the ability to make decisions aimed at the common good" (47.2). The Church can only exhort people in these democracies to reflect upon the truth and meaning of their views. The Church can help nations to develop their own particular cultures and ways of life through the witness, in word and deed, to the Gospel of Jesus Christ. It is in appealing to "man's heart" that the followers of Christ seek to influence culture (51.1), such as encouraging people to take responsibility for the well-being of their brothers and sisters (51.2), to pursue paths of peace instead of war and violence (52.1), and to promote development as the path to peace (52.2).

What riches the Lord has given to the Church through the "social teaching" of Pope John Paul II! This teaching was first presented in the encyclical on human work, *Laborem Exercens*, continued and developed in the encyclical *Sollicitudo Rei Socialis*, and is concluded in this final "social encyclical," *Centesimus Annus*. It is a treasure, which needs to be studied and applied.

QUESTIONS FOR REFLECTION

1. How has "a *correct view of the human person* and of his unique value" (11.3) guided the Church's social teaching?

2. Reflect on the inherent dangers in emphasizing economic development without "respect for the natural and fundamental right to know the truth and live according to that truth" (39.c).

3. As members of a developed (and wealthy) nation, what are the particular temptations we face in living the teaching that the goods of the earth are to be shared among all people?

4. Summarize *Centesimus Annus*' teaching on the importance of the State in the economic sector.

5. Summarize the Church's views toward the political and economic systems employed by the State, including the strengths and the dangers of modern forms of "socialism" and "capitalism" ("free market" economics).

FOR FURTHER READING

- Fr. Austin Fagothey, S.J., *Right and Reason*, Chapters 32 (Capitalism), 33 (Marxism)
- Pope Leo XIII, On Capital and Labor (*Rerum Novarum*)
- John Paul II, On Social Concerns (*Sollicitudo Rei Socialis*)
- John Paul II, On Human Work (*Laborem Exercens*)
- *Catechism*, 2402–2414; 2426–2449

10

Veritatis Splendor
"The Splendor of Truth"

The Tenth Encyclical Letter of Pope John Paul II

August 6, 1993

In this encyclical letter, John Paul II notes, "This is the first time, in fact, that the Magisterium of the Church has set forth in detail the fundamental elements of this teaching [regarding morality], and presented the principles for the pastoral discernment" (115.1). *Veritatis Splendor* is a groundbreaking document. It requires careful study, and its content is crucial for Catholics today to appropriate—especially the objective truth and unchanging nature of God's moral law in the face of increasing moral relativism.

THE CENTRAL SUBJECT

The title of the encyclical tells us that the subject with which we are dealing is that of *truth*. Human beings are made for truth. They burn with an innate desire to know the truth. Jesus Christ, of course, *is* the truth (Jn. 14:6), "the decisive answer to every one of man's questions, his religious and moral questions in particular" (2.2). The role of the Church, particularly her pastors, is therefore to proclaim and teach God's truth as revealed by Jesus and the Holy Spirit. And what the Church can teach about morality is particularly important because "it is precisely *on the path of the moral life that the way of salvation is open to all*" (3.2), even to those who through no fault of their own, do not yet know or believe in Jesus Christ as the Lord and the Truth.

ADDRESSING A CRISIS

All this, opening the encyclical letter, is very clear and positive. However, John Paul goes on to say that the encyclical's purpose is to recall "certain fundamental truths of Catholic doctrine, which…risk being distorted or denied" (4.2). No, it is not just a "risk": there is a *genuine crisis* of widespread questioning and even rejection of traditional moral doctrine and of the authority of the Catholic Church to speak with authority on moral issues.

It is said that the Church can, at best, "exhort consciences" and "propose values" for individuals to consider in making their own decisions and life choices. Pope John Paul notes that even in Catholic seminaries questions are raised concerning, for example, whether God's commandments are still binding. The suggestion is made that the unity of the Church is based on matters of faith (doctrine), but not on moral teaching and practice, where each individual must follow his or her own conscience.

Hence the purpose of this encyclical is to present the *principles* of the Church's moral teaching based on Sacred Scripture and Tradition (the teaching itself is presented in detail in the *Catechism of the Catholic Church*), and to discuss the phenomenon of dissent from the Church's moral teaching: its presuppositions and consequences.

FINDING THE GOOD LIFE

Chapter One of *Veritatis Splendor* reflects on the meaning of the rich young man's question to Jesus about how to attain eternal life: "Teacher, what good deed must I do . . .?" (see Mt. 19:16). He is most likely a devout Jew who knows the law (Torah), but he senses that Jesus has a fuller answer to his questions about the moral good and eternal life. These are questions that every person has at some point in life.

Jesus knows that these are, at root, *religious* questions, because their answer is found in God, who alone is goodness and fullness of life. They are also questions about the *purpose of human life*, which is *"to live 'for the praise of God's glory'"* (10.1; quoting Eph. 1:12). The good life—the moral life—consists in seeking God and in living as God lives, for we are created by God to be holy, as God is holy (cf. Lev. 19:2; 1 Pt. 1:15–16).

However, and here is the problem, *we are unable to do this on our own.* No human effort, by itself, can succeed in making us holy like God or in enabling us to keep any of God's laws. This can only come from a gift of God, which is received by following Jesus' invitation to "Come, follow me." (Mt. 19:21)

KNOWING AND FOLLOWING THE GOOD

The question of what good we must do is also answered by looking within ourselves, into our *hearts*, for there God has placed a law (cf. Rom. 2:15), which is called the "natural law." St. Thomas Aquinas taught that the natural law is an innate God-given understanding of what we should do and what to avoid. The commandments of the Old Covenant that God revealed to Moses are still a valid and explicit expression of God's law, and so Jesus tells the rich young man that the first 'good' he must do to attain eternal life is to keep the commandments. Keeping these commandments is "the *first necessary step on the journey towards freedom*, its starting-point" (13.4). He refers to St. Augustine who taught that keeping the commandments is "the beginning of freedom, not perfect freedom."

Now Pope John Paul shows us a deeper reality at the heart of the commandments. First of all, St. Paul stresses that the Ten Commandments—the "Decalogue," or "Ten Words"—are reflections of the great commandments to love God and to love our neighbor, as Jesus taught. We know that "love is the fulfilling of the Law" (Rom. 13:10). John Paul then points out that *"Jesus himself is the living 'fulfillment' of the Law...he himself becomes a living and personal Law* who invites people to follow him; through the Spirit, he gives the grace to share his own life and love" (15.2).

Christian morality is, thus, very personal. It is following and imitating Jesus Christ through the power and grace of the Holy Spirit. Pope John Paul II also says that the Christian moral life can be summed up by the eight Beatitudes (Mt. 5:3–12), which "are a sort of *self-portrait of Christ*," and therefore, "are *invitations to discipleship and communion of life with Christ*" (16.3).

THE PROBLEM AND THE PROMISE

Sadly the young man is unable to accept Jesus' invitation to "be perfect" by letting go of everything to follow Jesus. The power of "the flesh" is too strong (18.1). The encyclical makes it clear that Jesus' call to follow him, to be perfect, is not restricted to a small group, but is for everyone (cf. 18.2). The problem the young man faces is the problem each of us faces.

Lest we, like Jesus' disciples, become discouraged, or walk away like the rich young man, John Paul II reminds us once again that the foundation of Christian morality is not obeying commandments in some abstract fashion, but *"holding fast to the very person of Jesus"* (19.3), proceeding along the path of love: "Love one another as I have loved you," Jesus said (Jn. 15:12). *"Following Christ* is not an outward imitation,…[but] means *becoming conformed to him."* He then explains, "This is the *effect of grace,* of the active presence of the Holy Spirit in us" (21.1).

Because our life in Christ is a work of grace we can say, truly and happily, "with God all things are possible" (Mt. 19:26). To live and love as Christ did *is* possible by the gift received—"his Spirit, whose first 'fruit' (cf. Gal. 5:22) is charity" (22.3)—and *only* with this gift. As St. Thomas Aquinas taught, *"the New Law is the grace of the Holy Spirit given through faith in Christ"* (24.4). This implies that Christians possess something that those who do not know Christ do not have: his own presence and the fullness of the Spirit.

THE BEST TRUTH TO ANNOUNCE

Jesus promised his followers, the Church, "I am with you always" (25.1; quoting Mt. 28:20). The Church is the "pillar and bulwark of the truth" (27.3; quoting 1 Tim. 3:5), of the full truth about who Jesus is and in what life in him consists. She has received a mission and a responsibility, which entails proclaiming and defending the truth regarding moral action and behavior. It is within her 'living Tradition' that the authentic interpretation of the Lord's law develops, with the help of the Holy Spirit.

Thus Pope John Paul concludes this opening chapter of *Veritatis Splendor* with the reminder that this law of Love, found in Jesus Christ and made possible by his grace, the Holy Spirit, is part of the truth that Jesus gave his people, the Church, to announce and to defend.

Perhaps the best summary of the first chapter is the following:

The moral prescriptions which God imparted in the Old Covenant, and which attained their perfection in the New and Eternal Covenant in the very person of the Son of God made man, **must be** *faithfully kept and continually put into practice* in the various different cultures throughout the course of history. The task of interpreting these prescriptions was entrusted by Jesus to the Apostles and to their successors, with the special assistance of the Spirit of truth: "He who hears you hears me" (Lk. 10:16). By the light and the strength this Spirit the Apostles carried out their mission of preaching the Gospel and of pointing out the "way" of the Lord (cf. Acts 18:25), teaching above all how to follow and imitate Christ: "For to me to live is Christ" (Phil. 1:21). (25.2; bold emphasis mine)

FREEDOM AND CONSCIENCE

The second chapter of *Veritatis Splendor* focuses on the challenges to specific areas of the moral teaching of the Church in some contemporary streams of moral theology. Scholars, John Paul reminds us, are to seek the renewal of moral theology, and this must always be consistent with "sound teaching" (2 Tim. 4:3). The Church "does not intend to impose…any particular theological system" (29.4), for she proclaims doctrine and not particular theologies. The *Magisterium* has the responsibility, therefore, to provide the measure for all proposed theologies by teaching the principles of sound doctrine and warning against moral teachings or systems that violate these principles.

Many of the current debates center around the issue of religious freedom and "freedom of conscience." Pope John Paul II emphasizes that freedom and conscience must always be seeking and conformed to truth, which is objective and thus cannot be reduced to criteria such as a person's sincerity, authenticity and "being at peace with oneself" (32.1). There is a "fundamental dependence of freedom upon truth," which is expressed in Jesus' teaching that, "If you continue in my word, . . . you will know the truth, and the truth will make you free" (Jn. 8:31–32) (cf. 34.3). In short, true freedom is freedom to discover the truth and to live according to it once it is found.

Following this introduction, the chapter is devoted to three topics: Freedom and Law (35–53), Conscience and Truth (54–65), and the concept of "Fundamental Choice or Option" (65–70), followed by a concluding section summarizing the nature of the moral act (71–83).

OBJECTIVE MORALITY, FREEDOM AND THE LAW

The first section explores the *"alleged conflict between freedom and law"* (35.3). Some today see human freedom and God's law (either natural or revealed) as opposed to each other, particularly because obedience to God's law seems to limit human freedom, imposing an extraneous authority from the outside ("heteronomy"). John Paul II explains that human freedom finds it true meaning and fulfillment when "human reason and human will participate in God's wisdom and providence" (41.2). Obedience to God's law is like discovering and following light in a dark place, leading the person who follows the light to Light itself—God and his Kingdom! St. Thomas Aquinas said that the natural law is nothing else "but an imprint on us of the divine light" (42.2). This "light" also enables the person, enlightened by it, to correctly discern good from evil, which is carried out by "*reason, in particular by…reason enlightened by Divine Revelation and by faith*" (44.2).

As St. Paul tells us, "where the Spirit of the Lord is, there is freedom" (45.1; cf. 2 Cor. 3:17). So the opposition between freedom and God's law is shown to be false. True freedom is the fulfillment of our nature, acting and living as God created us to live. This is discovered through both the law of human nature (*natural law*) that can be known through right reason, and more fully through the moral law that God has revealed, first in the Old Covenant and now brought to fulfillment through the teaching of Jesus and the Holy Spirit dwelling within.

However, many people today, including moral theologians, deny either the existence or the specificity of the *natural* moral laws, and argue that "man, as a rational being, not only can but actually *must freely determine the meaning of his behavior*" (47). Pope John Paul takes up this issue in detail, arguing that there *is* a human nature that God created "in the beginning" with a specific moral dimension that is not determined by humans: there is a human nature that is not dependent on peoples' culture nor upbringing, nor psychological or sociological factors. There are, he argues, "objective norms of morality" (53.1; cf. *GS* 16). This means that human freedom can either be used properly (observing and following these norms) or improperly (ignoring or rejecting these norms). Humans have freedom, but, as in the beginning, this freedom can be used either for good or for evil. God and his laws both determine and reveal what good and evil are.

Pope John Paul II acknowledged that the Church must continue "to seek out and to discover *the most adequate formulation* for universal and permanent moral norms in the light of different cultural contexts…This truth of moral law—like that of the 'deposit of faith'—unfolds down the centuries"

(53.3). There are new questions and new insights that give rise to a fuller understanding and articulation of the universal moral law over time. Believers and theologians contribute to this. It is the role of the Church's *Magisterium* to discern these and then to proclaim those that are true expressions of the moral law.

CONSCIENCE AND TRUTH

This section of *Veritatis Splendor* contrasts two views of conscience: on the one hand, the traditional view beautifully presented in Vatican II's *Gaudium et Spes* (16) that conscience discerns or judges how objective moral norms (i.e. the moral law) are to be applied rightly by the person in particular situations; and on the other hand, the more recent "creative" understanding of conscience in which conscience considers what ought to be done in each situation with moral norms seen as "guidelines" but not as absolute or unbreakable moral "laws." Conscience, in this second view, functions as a "higher law" which each person is bound to follow, regardless of what "objective" laws say.

THE BIBLICAL VIEW OF CONSCIENCE

Pope John Paul II contends that this "creative" understanding of conscience is opposed to the biblical one. Conscience, in Scripture, is a "witness," which "in a certain sense confronts man with the law" showing him either his faithfulness or unfaithfulness to it (57.2). Furthermore, he points out that conscience is not just an interior "dialogue" within a person about what is right or wrong, but "it is also a *dialogue of man with God*, the author of the law…Moral conscience…opens [the person] to the call, the *voice* of God" (58). Conscience, therefore, is not a "creative" work of a person to determine the truth about what to do in a particular circumstance, but is a listening to the voice of God within. St. Paul taught that "what the law requires is written on their [the Gentiles'] hearts, while their conscience also bears witness and their conflicting thoughts accuse or perhaps excuse them…on that day when…God judges the secrets of men by Christ Jesus" (57.1, 59.1; quoting Rom. 2:14–15, 16).

Conscience, does not, therefore, free one from law in order for a person to make an autonomous, independent decision. Conscience applies the natural moral law, the law "written on the hearts," to a particular case, and expresses within the person a judgment about the truth: what is the right or the wrong thing to do in accordance with the moral law inscribed within the person.

The Church has always pointed out that a person's conscience can err: it "*is not an infallible judge*" (62.3). Hence we need to make the laborious (but fruitful) effort to form our conscience: "to make it the object of a continuous conversion to what is true and to what is good" (64.1). (Also see *Dominum et Vivificantem*, nos. 42–45 on the Holy Spirit as the "light of consciences" and "laborious effort of conscience" necessary to discover and follow God's Law.)

Pope John Paul reminds us of the title Scripture text of this chapter: "not to be conformed to the mentality of this world, but to *be transformed* [emphasis mine] by the renewal of our mind (cf. Rom 12:2): It is the 'heart' converted to the Lord and to the love of what is good which is really the source of *true* judgments of conscience" (64.1).

FORMING CONSCIENCE

Finally, Pope John Paul notes that our greatest help in forming our consciences is the Church and her *Magisterium*, "For the Catholic Church is by the will of Christ the teacher of truth" (64.2). Some think that conscience must be free from *external* authority, but "when she [the Church] pronounces on moral questions, [this] in no way undermines the freedom of conscience of Christians" (Ibid). Freedom is not freedom *from* the truth, but freedom *in* the truth, which the Church exists to proclaim. Let us listen, finally to John Paul's striking words on this subject:

> The Church puts herself always and only at the *service of conscience*, helping it to avoid being tossed to and fro by every wind of doctrine proposed by human deceit (cf. Eph. 4:14), and helping it not to swerve from the truth about the good of man, but rather, especially in more difficult questions, to attain the truth with certainty and to abide in it. (64.2)

FUNDAMENTAL OPTION AND MORTAL SIN

A controversial topic that Pope John Paul II addresses in Chapter 2 of *Veritatis Splendor* is the modern theological concept of "fundamental choice" or "fundamental option." The biblical basis for this notion is the "obedience of faith" (cf. Rom. 16:26) by which a person entrusts his whole self to God (66.1; cf. *DV* 5). In the Old Testament, Israel's fundamental decision is whom they will obey or serve. "Choose this day," Joshua urges the people, "whom you will serve!"

(Josh. 24:15). "The morality of the New Covenant is similarly dominated by the fundamental call of Jesus to follow him," as in the invitation he gives to the young man (66.1; cf. Mt. 19:21). We have the freedom to respond to that call to serve the Lord, but as St. Paul warns, "do not use your freedom as an opportunity for the flesh" (66.2; quoting Gal. 5:13). Some theologians have proposed that one's *fundamental option* for God would not necessarily be altered by a particular act, even by a mortal sin. Pope John Paul, however, defends the tradition that one's fundamental option is directly affected by every moral decision. He states, "With every freely committed mortal sin,…even if he perseveres in faith, he loses 'sanctifying grace,' 'charity' and 'eternal happiness'" (68.2).

Here, as elsewhere in this section, Pope John Paul refers to his 1984 apostolic exhortation on Reconciliation and Penance (17). Hence, while the idea and language of *fundamental choice* or *fundamental option* may certainly describe one's basic orientation toward God—either of faith and fidelity, or unbelief and infidelity—it must also be understood that particular acts have specific moral consequences. For example, it must be remembered that even one mortal sin separates a person from God and results in the loss of eternal life if the sin is unrepented. To think otherwise would be to undermine the seriousness of our actions.

PROPORTIONALISM

In the final section of Chapter 2, the Pope evaluates two very popular moral systems known as "proportionalism" and "consequentialism." Both of these moral systems might be seen as forms of "situation ethics." Although there are a variety of approaches that the Pope considers here, we can say briefly that these theories seek to judge the moral value of an act by assessing the foreseen consequences of the act, and whether in these consequences a greater *proportion* of the results are good or evil. These systems invariably place greater weight on the person's intention and the circumstances that influence the choice to act rather than on the objective moral character of the act (which is sometimes disputed). How, it is asked, can an act be evil if the person acts, even against a specific moral precept, motivated exclusively by "faithfulness…to the highest values of charity and prudence" (75.3)? According to this view, specific moral norms or precepts are "always relative and open to exceptions" (Ibid).

Pope John Paul points out the weaknesses of these positions. On the practical level, it is impossible to foresee all the possible consequences of an act, or indeed even to know them after the act is performed. On the moral level, the Pope stresses that *"the morality of the human act depends primarily and fundamentally on the 'object' rationally chosen by the deliberate will"* (78.1). Is the act itself—intrinsically—right or wrong, good or evil? This is primarily moral judgment. Further, acts that are intrinsically evil (that is, evil in themselves) may *never* be done for a "good intention"—"to do evil that good [or a *greater good*] may come of it" (79–82; cf. Rom 3:8).

A clear presentation of why certain positions are in error is only, however, a first step. Though this chapter warns against the "dangers of certain ethical theories," the first duty of the Church is to "show the inviting splendor of that truth which is Jesus Christ himself." By following Jesus and responding to the gift of the Holy Spirit, "we are enabled to interiorize the law, to receive it and to live it as the motivating force of true personal freedom" (83.2).

TRUE FREEDOM

The true meaning of freedom in the moral life is summarized in the third chapter: "only the freedom which submits to the Truth leads the human person to his true good. The good of the person is to be in the Truth and to *do* the Truth" (84.2).

Tragically, he says, "this essential bond between Truth, the Good and Freedom has been largely lost sight of by present-day culture." This is why the mission of the Church is so important—the Church can help people to discover the wisdom of God in which the unity between truth, freedom and good is recognized. Jesus Christ, who is Truth, is himself the key which opens the door to this discovery, and in this third chapter the Pope draws our attention particularly to Christ crucified. *"The Crucified Christ reveals the authentic meaning of freedom: he lives it fully in the total gift of himself* and calls his disciples to share in his freedom" (85). As implied here, the freedom of the follower of Christ is the freedom to *give* of himself, even to the point of death.

There are no "moral short-cuts" that enable the follower of Jesus Christ to avoid the Cross—the sacrifice of obeying God and the moral law. "Through the moral life, faith becomes 'confession',…it becomes *witness*" (89.2). The ultimate witness is that of the martyr, and Pope John Paul recalls Susanna, John the Baptist, the deacon Stephen and James the Apostle (cf. 91) as examples of those numerous saints who were ready to give their lives in witness to the truth. They were ready to die rather than to commit any act morally evil in itself, thus reawakening the moral sense of their age and dispelling, by their lives, any confusion between good and evil (which the Pope calls "the most dangerous crisis that can afflict man"). Even though a few are normally called to be martyrs, all Christians today are called to a "sometimes heroic commitment" to be faithful to God in moral decisions every day. This requires the virtue of fortitude and calling on God's grace in prayer both for courage and clarity of conscience (cf. 93.1–2).

DEMOCRACY AND TOTALITARIANISM

This courage and clarity is also needed to apply and follow moral norms in the social and political orders. Civil authorities are not exempt from observing the moral law and applying it faithfully in their spheres of influence—there are no exceptions for *any* individuals or groups from observing and following the moral law.

The Pope shakes us out of our complacency by reminding us that it is not only atheistic and totalitarian states that can oppose the moral law, especially with regard to the dignity and rights of each person. Pope John Paul prophetically warned of *"the risk of an alliance between democracy and ethical relativism,* which would remove any sure moral reference point from political and social life, and on a deeper level make the acknowledgment of truth impossible" (101.1). He continues:

> If there is no ultimate truth to guide and direct political activity, then ideas and convictions can easily be manipulated for reasons of power. As history demonstrates, a democracy without values easily turns into open or thinly disguised totalitarianism. (101.1; cf. *CA* 46)

Thus, it is the Church's task and mission to tirelessly proclaim the moral law.

"Evangelization—and therefore the 'new evangelization'—*also involves the proclamation and presentation of morality"* (107.1). This must not just be a message proclaimed, but also lived in the holiness of God's people. The life of holiness is made possible by the grace of the sacraments, especially the Eucharist, and through the strength and inspiration of the Holy Spirit (cf. 108). Moral theologians are challenged to resist the current trends of ethical and moral relativism and instead elucidate, in union with the Magisterium, the truth and wisdom of the moral teaching that has been handed down in the Church's tradition (cf. 109).

THE CHURCH'S RESPONSIBILITY

In all of this, how can we sum up the responsibility laid before the Church? Pope John Paul says that the Church has a responsibility, before God and humanity, to preserve and witness to the full truth of the Gospel of Jesus Christ. This will not always be easy for in doing this the Church "is not infrequently seen as the sign of intolerable intransigence, particularly with regard to the enormously complex and conflict-filled situations present in the moral life of individuals and of society today" (95.1). Some say that this stance contradicts the Church's role as mother, full of understanding and compassion. But the Holy Father points out that "genuine understanding and compassion must mean love for the person, for his true good, for his authentic freedom." And this does not result, he says, from concealing or weakening the moral truth but from proposing it "as an outpouring of God's eternal wisdom, which we have received in Christ" (95.2). A good mother will always direct her children to the truth and warn them to avoid evil.

It is impossible to sum up this hugely significant encyclical in a few lines, but we can probably do no better than to conclude with the heartfelt prayer Pope John Paul II makes to Our Lady at the close of the Letter:

> O Mary,
> Mother of Mercy,
> watch over all people,
> that the Cross of Christ
> may not be emptied of its power,
> that man may not stray|
> from the path of the good
> or become blind to sin,
> but may put his hope ever more fully in God
> who is "rich in mercy" (Eph. 2:4).
> May he carry out the good works prepared
> by God beforehand (cf. Eph. 2:10)
> and so live completely
> "for the praise of his glory" (Eph. 1:12).

—————————— QUESTIONS FOR REFLECTION ——————————

1. What are the needs and questions addressed in this document?

2. Consider the role of the Ten Commandments and the Beatitudes in living the moral life. How is living this life made possible?

3. What are the "links" or relationship between an understanding of truth (which is objective), objective norms of morality, and human freedom?

4. What are the role of the conscience and the place of the Church and her Magisterium in forming consciences?

5. How can a clear understanding of certain acts, which have specific moral content (i.e. that many acts are intrinsically good or evil, right or wrong), be an antidote against moral confusion in today's society?

6. What does Pope John Paul II see as the Church's role and responsibility concerning Truth and the Moral Law?

FOR FURTHER READING

- Fr. Austin Fagothey, S.J., *Right and Reason*, Chapters 5 (Conscience), 6 (Good), 12 (Law), 14 (Freedom), 15 (Situation)
- Benedict XVI, *Jesus of Nazareth*
- *Catechism*, Part III: Life In Christ
- *USCCA*, Chapter 31 (Do Not Steal; Act Justly)

11

Evangelium Vitae
"The Gospel of Life"

The Eleventh Encyclical Letter of Pope John Paul II

March 25, 1995

"The Gospel of Life is at the heart of Jesus' message" (1.1). This opening line of Pope John Paul II's eleventh encyclical letter makes it clear that Catholics are called to be "unconditionally pro-life" (28.1). This document explains with prophetic force, based on both faith and reason, *what* this means and *why* it is an essential aspect of Catholic faith and identity. The fact that many people view this pro-life stance as "rigid" or "narrow-minded" reflects the cultural climate of our times.

THE VALUE AND DIGNITY OF HUMAN LIFE

That each human person is "priceless"—of inestimable value and dignity—is the basic premise of the "Gospel of Life." This is a "natural law written in the heart" (2.2; cf. Rom. 2:14–15)—a truth to which the conscience of each person testifies, despite powerful coordinated efforts to suppress or distort this truth. However, "The Gospel of God's love for man, the Gospel of the dignity of the human person and the Gospel of life are a single indivisible Gospel" (2.4).

Pope John Paul II notes that the Catholic Church has spoken out directly and consistently against all crimes against life and human dignity (cf. *GS* 27). Unfortunately, he sees this tragic state of affairs expanding, not lessening, with scientific advances. Significantly, the biblical text that John Paul chooses as the basis for his reflections on "present-day threats to human life" is Cain's killing of his brother, Abel (Gen. 4:2–6) in which the Lord says, "The voice of your brother's blood is crying to me from the ground" (Gen. 4:10; *EV* 10).

The first truth that the modern world must hear and heed is that there is a God who judges this and all crimes against life and will not let any of them go unpunished (cf. 8.5; 9:1). "Whoever attacks human life, in some way attacks God himself," the author of life (9.1). Yes, God is also merciful; he puts a mark on Cain to protect him from being killed ("not even a murderer loses his personal dignity" 9.3), but he is responsible for his crime. Yet, Cain does not think so, and neither does the modern world acknowledge its guilt for many crimes against life. When God asked Cain, "What have you done?" John Paul II believes that this question "is addressed also to the people of today, to make them realize the extent and gravity of the attacks against life which continue to mark human history" (10.2). What are these "crimes" (10.4)?

- "The violence against life done to millions of human beings, especially children, who are forced into poverty, malnutrition and hunger because of an unjust distribution of resources"

- "The violence inherent not only in wars as such but in the scandalous arms trade, which spawns [violence]"

- "Reckless tampering with the world's ecological balance"

- "The criminal spread of drugs"

- "The promotion of certain kinds of sexual activity which, besides being morally unacceptable, also involve grave risks to life"

THE SACREDNESS OF HUMAN LIFE IN ECLIPSE

Pope John Paul observes that the value of life today is undergoing a kind of "eclipse" (11.3) with the emergence of a "culture of death" (12), which involves a "war of the powerful against the weak." This war not only includes the oppression of the economically weak—the poor—but the rejection of life that is "unwanted" through abortion and contraception, which "are often closely connected, as fruits of the same tree" (13.3); through prenatal diagnosis (if used to procure "eugenic abortions"), infanticide and euthanasia. Even techniques of artificial reproduction "which would seem to be at the service of life...actually open the door to new threats against life," such as the inevitable destruction of "spare embryos" which "reduces human life to the level of simple 'biological material' to be freely disposed of" (14.1).

Euthanasia, which appears to be based on compassion, has the double difficulty of failing "to perceive any meaning or value in suffering" (15.2) and (worse) is based on "a certain Promethean attitude which leads people to think that they can control life and death by taking the decisions about them into their own hands" (15.3).

What do we say, however, to those who view taking on these decisions about life and death as inevitable and noble, who perceive humanity reaching a "new stage" in which we are taking responsibility for ourselves and our destiny? One might, first, look at the fruit of the twentieth century, which John Paul summarizes as "an era of massive attacks on life, an endless series of wars and a continual taking of innocent human life" (17.2). Secondly, those who wish to take on the responsibility to make decisions about life and death are often basing their judgments on criteria of efficiency and utility: "Thus it is proposed to eliminate malformed babies, the severely handicapped, the disabled, the elderly, especially when they are not self-sufficient, and the terminally ill" (15.3). The same utilitarian motives conspire to limit and regulate life at its beginning by "carrying out actual campaigns to make contraception, sterilization and abortion widely available" in what is tantamount to "an objective 'conspiracy against life'" (17.2).

THE MEANING OF FREEDOM

Pope John Paul also sees as a root cause of the anti-life mentality a distorted notion of freedom "which exalts the isolated individual in an absolute way, and gives no place to solidarity, to openness to others and service of them... which ends up by becoming the freedom of 'the strong' against the weak who have no choice but to submit" (19.3). This is illustrated in Cain's response when God asks him about his brother: "Am I my brother's keeper?" (Gen. 4:9). *Freedom* becomes a "cover" for self-centered individualism; we have *freedom* to do whatever we want to advance our own interests. As a result of this, on the societal level Pope John Paul observes that "rather than societies of 'people living together', our cities risk becoming societies of people who are rejected, marginalized, uprooted and oppressed" (18.5). Instead of welcoming and supporting the poor, the weak, the unborn, we seek ways to keep them *in line* or to eliminate them. John Paul notes in today's world "a surprising contradiction. Precisely in an age when the inviolable rights of the person are solemnly proclaimed and the value of life is publicly affirmed, the very right to life is being denied or trampled upon, especially at...the moment of birth and the moment of death" (18.3).

Even in democratic regimes which claim to defend fundamental human rights (the "right to life" being the most basic) and human dignity, this principle "is betrayed in its very foundations: 'How is it possible to speak of the dignity of every human person when the killing of the weakest and most innocent is permitted? In the name of what justice is the most unjust of discriminations practiced...?'" (20.2). "To claim the right to abortion, infanticide and euthanasia, and to recognize that right in law, means to attribute to human freedom a perverse and evil significance: that of an absolute power over others and against others. This is the death of true freedom" (20.3).

THE STATE AND HUMAN RIGHTS

Pope John Paul II makes absolutely clear that no government can legitimately revoke or overturn fundamental human rights, beginning with the right to life. If a democracy claims to do this on the basis of a vote or a court decision, the State "moves toward a form of totalitarianism. The State is no longer the 'common home' where all can live together on the basis of principles of fundamental equality, but it is transformed into a tyrant State, which arrogates to itself the right to dispose of the life of the weakest and most defenseless members, from the unborn child to the elderly, in the name of a public interest which is nothing but the interest of one part" (20.2). John Paul II goes on to explain that while the State may insist on the "legality" of these laws permitting abortion and euthanasia, "what we have here is only the tragic caricature of legality; the democratic ideal, which is only truly such when it acknowledges and safeguards the dignity of every human person, is betrayed in its very foundations" (20.2).

This analysis by our late, great Holy Father confronts us with the monumental struggle that Christians must recognize and take upon ourselves. God told Cain that because of his sin God would hide his face from him (cf. Gen. 4:14). Our society, too, is suffering an eclipse of the sense of God, in "a social and cultural climate dominated by secularism" (21.1):

Those who allow themselves to be influenced by this climate easily fall into a sad vicious circle: when the sense of God is lost, there is also a tendency to lose the sense of man. (21.1)

THE DARKENING LANDSCAPE

The result is a "progressive darkening of the capacity to discern God's living and saving presence" (21.1). If God is lost, *life* itself is no longer seen as a "splendid gift of God, something 'sacred' entrusted to his responsibility...and 'veneration'. Life itself becomes a mere 'thing', which man claims as his exclusive property, completely subject to his control and manipulation" (22.1). Man "busies himself with programming, controlling and dominating birth and death. Birth and death, instead of being primary experiences demanding to be 'lived' become things to be merely 'possessed' or 'rejected'" (22.2). Nature is no longer "*mater*" (mother) but only "matter," and is "subjected to every kind of manipulation" (22.3). Suffering "is 'censored', rejected as useless, indeed opposed as an evil, always and in every way to be avoided" (23.2). The body is purely material, and sexuality is a somatic function, a means of satisfaction rather than a sign of mutual self-giving and accepting of another in their richness as persons. The unitive and procreative meanings of human sexuality are artificially separated, with procreation subject to control as either an "enemy" to be avoided or something to be demanded "at the right time" instead of signifying "the complete acceptance of the other and therefore an openness to the richness of life which the child represents" (23.3).

A BLEAK PICTURE

Pope John Paul II completes the first twenty-four articles of his encyclical on the Gospel of Life with an observation of St. Paul on his own time:

> A large part of contemporary society looks sadly like that humanity which Paul describes in his Letter to the Romans. It is composed "of men who by their wickedness suppress the truth" (1:18): having denied God and believing they can build the earthly city without him, "they become futile in their thinking" so that "their senseless minds were darkened" (1:21). (24.1)

The "eclipse of the sense of God and of man" is affecting both individual consciences and the "moral conscience" of society. With the "penetrating influence" of the media assisting, the moral conscience of individuals and society is subjected "to an extremely serious and mortal danger: that of confusion between good and evil, precisely in relation to the fundamental right to life" (24.1). It is evident in our debates about life issues that there is no societal consensus on what is right and wrong, not even whether there is objective truth to be found in these matters.

SIGNS OF HOPE AND CHALLENGE

While the first part of *Evangelium Vitae* analyzes the contemporary situation, focusing on the "culture of death" and the moral blindness regarding life issues afflicting the modern world, there is hope. The Gospel, the Good News of Christ, ever rises on the horizon. Specific signs of hope flowing from faith in Christ include

- married couples who are fully open to life;

- centers in support of life and volunteers who support those in need when human life is jeopardized;

- advances in medical science that can protect the unborn and heal or help those suffering;

- movements to raise social awareness in defense of life;

- opposition to war as an instrument for resolution of conflicts;

- opposition to the death penalty;

- concern for ecology, improving the quality of life;

- the development and spread of bioethics, providing moral guidance in issues concerning human life; and finally,

- "all those daily gestures of openness, sacrifice and unselfish care which countless people lovingly make in families, hospitals, orphanages, homes for the elderly and other centers or communities which defend life" (27.2).

In this critical conflict, *God charges everyone* "with the inescapable responsibility of choosing to be unconditionally pro-life" (28.1). Jesus' teaching about the dignity and sacredness of human life is clear. It includes "everything that human experience and reason tell us about the value of human life" (30.2).

THE GOSPEL OF LIFE

The first premise of this "Gospel of Life" is that "[Human] Life is always a good" (34.1), because it reflects and shows forth the goodness of its Creator: God. Humans are made in God's "image and likeness," and St. Irenaeus in the second century, remarked that man, fully alive, "is the glory of God" (34.2). Tragically, sin has tarnished the image of God in man, but for those who have committed themselves to following Christ, in them "the divine image is restored, renewed, and brought to perfection"—fulfilling God's desire that all "should 'be conformed to the image of his [God's] Son' (Rom. 8:29)" (36.4). Christians know *that human life is sacred* because it has its *origin* in God, its *restoration* to the image of God made possible through the redeeming work of Jesus Christ, and its glorious *destiny* set before it—to have an eternal life of loving union with God. St. Irenaeus wrote of this destiny when he taught "the life of man consists in the vision of God" (*Adversus Haereses*, IV, 207).

HUMAN RESPONSIBILITY TOWARD LIFE

God has lavished the gift of life, both physical and spiritual, on human beings. With this gift comes the responsibility to honor and respect it. Humans are not the "lords" of human life: God is, and only God can determine when a life should begin and end. God does this with a "loving concern for his creatures" (39.3). Although the Old Testament allowed severe corporal punishment and death penalty, even the ancient Hebrews legislated for the defense of weak and innocent life, including children in the womb (41.2; cf. Ex. 21:22; 22:20–26).

With Jesus "these positive requirements assume new force and urgency" (41.2). For example, in the parable of the Good Samaritan, we see how the Samaritan takes responsibility for the life and care of a total stranger in need. Jesus even calls people to love their enemies (cf. Mt. 5:38–48) and do good to them (cf. Lk. 6:27, 33, 35). At the heart of Jesus' teaching on human life is "the requirement to show reverence and love for every person and the life of every person" (41.4). This is a dimension of what it means for humans to have dominion over the earth (Gen. 1:28)—every human being is to be a "steward" or "caretaker" of life, especially human life (42.1–43.1).

THE GIFT OF LIFE

Evangelium Vitae teaches that responsibility for life "reaches its highest point in the giving of life through procreation by man and woman in marriage" (43.1). In this a couple participates directly in God's creative work by bringing forth a person who bears God's image and likeness (43.2). Pope John Paul here stresses that this event is more than a biological event or project, for "God Himself is present in human fatherhood and motherhood" in a totally unique way. God alone is the source of that image and likeness which is transmitted by the creation of the immortal soul (43.2). Human beings, from the moment of conception, are not like any other animals, and certainly are not merely *biological material* that can be manipulated and disposed of at will, because God creates and bestows on the person at that moment a *soul*. Through the soul, the person possesses a spiritual life, a spiritual nature, and an eternal destiny that is in full union with, but transcends, the material or biological aspect of the person. While parents in conceiving a child "become partners in a divine undertaking" (43.4), the Holy Father stresses that "the task of accepting and serving life involves everyone" especially when life is at its weakest and most vulnerable—at the beginning and end of life and in times of sickness and distress (43.5, 44.1).

The remainder of Chapter 2 surveys the biblical texts that speak of the protection and service of life: "Before I formed you in the womb I knew you" (Jer. 1:5) marks the beginning of life, while Psalm 71:18 reflects on the end of life "so even to old age and gray hairs, O God, do not forsake me."

Yet Pope John Paul observes that there are no Scripture passages directly calling for the *protection* of life not yet born or life nearing its end. Why is this? It is because "the mere possibility of harming, attacking, or actually denying life in these circumstances is completely foreign to [their] religious and cultural way of thinking" (44.1). The Jewish people saw numerous offspring as a blessing, and venerated the elderly, even in their weakness and suffering. How far have we "progressed," using scientific advances routinely to kill unborn children and the elderly with quiet efficiency? Yet, God has inscribed a "law of life" in human hearts (cf. 49.1)—the truth that life is a gift from the Creator, who is the "absolute master" of any decision over life or death (cf. 47.3).

MEDITATION ON THE CROSS OF CHRIST

Our hope for the ultimate victory of "the Gospel of Life" rests only in Jesus Christ. Pope John Paul II closes Chapter 2 of *Evangelium Vitae* with a meditation on Jesus surrendering his human life on the Cross of Calvary, offering his life "as a ransom for many" (Mk. 10:45). In this act, Jesus both conquers death, sending forth new life—the gift of the Holy Spirit—to humanity (51.2) and teaches us the purpose and meaning of life, which is radical *service*. Service means laying down our lives for others, as Jesus did throughout his earthly life, reaching its climax on Calvary. The Pope says, "In this way Jesus proclaims that life finds its center, its meaning and its fulfillment when it is given up" (51.6). God has given us life, both natural and spiritual, and we are to share that life with others, as Jesus did, in sacrificial love and service.

GOD'S HOLY LAW REGARDING LIFE

The Catholic teaching on human life is based on God's laws or commandments, which present to us clear, objective truth, that are inscribed in our consciences and revealed in fullness and precision in Sacred Scripture and in the living Tradition of the Church which flows from Scripture. We have seen the Catholic teaching on life is "joyful good news" (52.2) because it protects and proclaims the sacredness of human life as God's gift. God's commandment regarding life is an expression of his love. It is also an "exacting task," for people must use their freedom to obey it (Ibid). Yes, human beings have dominion over the earth, but Pope John Paul reminds us that this rule is "not absolute, but ministerial…a real reflection of the unique and infinite lordship of God. Hence man must exercise it with wisdom and love…[which] comes about through obedience to God's holy Law" (52.3).

The "heart" of the third chapter of *Evangelium Vitae* is a presentation of God's law as it pertains especially to the beginning and end of human life. Pope John Paul refers to three sources in particular in this presentation:

- the *Catechism of the Catholic Church* (1992),

- the Declaration on Euthanasia (*Iura et Bona,* May 5, 1980), and

- the Instruction on Respect for Human Life (*Donum Vitae,* Feb. 22, 1987).

Donum Vitae summarizes the basic moral principle: "no one can, in any circumstance, claim for himself the right to destroy directly an innocent human being" (53.1; cf. *DVit* 5).

Human life is "sacred and inviolable," and "for this reason God will severely judge every violation of the commandment 'You shall not kill'" (53.3). The writings of the early Church (such as the *Didache*, "the most ancient non-biblical Christian writing") and other Christian sources (such as writing of Athenagoras and Tertullian) corroborate this (54.2).

"PARADOXICAL" APPLICATIONS

John Paul II discusses two situations "in which values proposed by God's law seem to involve a genuine paradox" (55.1): legitimate defense and the death penalty. The case of legitimate defense is paradoxical because it may result in the necessity, or even the duty, to take the life of another in order to preserve one's own life, or the lives of other innocent victims of unjust attack or aggression. The *Catechism of the Catholic Church* states, "legitimate defense can be not only a right but a grave duty for someone responsible for another's life, the common good of the family or of the State" (55.2; *Catechism*, no. 2265).

Even the Church had viewed the death penalty as a just punishment for certain capital crimes in the past. Today the Catholic Church calls for a more careful evaluation and concludes that society "ought not go to the extreme of executing the offender except...when it would not be possible otherwise to defend society. Today, however, as a result of steady improvements in the... penal system, such cases are very rare, if not practically non-existent" (56.2; cf. *Catechism*, no. 2267).

Both of these cases deal with the application of the commandment "thou shalt not kill" to capital criminals and unjust aggressors, but the Pope says this commandment "has absolute value when it refers to the innocent person. And all the more so in the case of weak and defenseless human beings, who find their ultimate defense against the arrogance and caprice of others only in the absolutely binding force of God's commandment" (57.1).

THE ABSOLUTE PROHIBITION OF KILLING OF THE INNOCENT

The core of God's law regarding the killing of the innocent is clear and straightforward:

The direct and voluntary killing of an innocent human being is always gravely immoral (57.4).

[It] can never be licit either as an end in itself or as a means to a good end. It is in fact a grave act of disobedience to the moral law, and indeed to God himself, the author and guarantor of that law; it contradicts the fundamental virtues of justice and charity. "Nothing and no one can in anyway permit the killing of an innocent human being, whether a fetus or an embryo, an infant or an adult, an old person, or one suffering from an incurable disease, or a person who is dying. Furthermore, no one is permitted to ask for this act of killing, either for himself or herself or for another person entrusted to his or her care, nor can he or she consent to it, either explicitly or implicitly. Nor can any authority legitimately recommend or permit such an action." (57.5; cf. *IB* II)

The two main cases considered of such direct killing are abortion and euthanasia. If the consistent teaching of Sacred Scripture and the Sacred Tradition of the Church on these issues seems to be "rigid" or unbending, it is because, first, we are dealing with God's law, not a human law, and, secondly, because (as stated above) this law is the only defense of innocent lives, especially in a time (today) when this law is being widely challenged, rejected or ignored.

In this book, I will not provide a complete summary of *Evangelium Vitae* on those subjects, but rather highlight a few significant points made.

- Regarding abortion, we need to avoid ambiguous terminology and call what is being done by its proper name (58.2).

- Modern genetic science confirms that "from the time that the ovum is fertilized [i.e. the moment of conception], a life is begun which is neither that of the father nor the mother; it is rather the life of a new human being with his own growth" (60.1). Thus, "fetus" and "embryo" are names for the stages of development of a human being, not of "biological material."

- The killing of an absolutely innocent, utterly weak and defenseless human being is properly called murder (58.3), a crime that the Catholic Church calls "unspeakable" (62.1) and "most serious and dangerous" (62.2).

- While the decision to have an abortion is often tragic and painful for the mother, no reason can ever justify the deliberate killing of an innocent human being (58.4).

- Responsibility for the death of an unborn child rests on everyone who contributes to the decision or the execution of the decision to kill the child, which may include the mother (58.4), the father of the child, family or "friends" whose influence contribute to the decision to abort the child, doctors and nurses who perform or assist in the killing (59.1), administrators of facilities where abortions are performed (59.2), legislators who promote and approve abortion laws, "those who have encouraged the spread of an attitude of sexual permissiveness and a lack of esteem for motherhood," and international institutions which promote or support the legalization and spread of abortion world-wide (59.2).

- The automatic excommunication of Catholics who procure an abortion, knowing the penalty, and of their accomplices, is intended to lead the persons who abort to become aware of the gravity of their deed and to foster conversion and repentance (62.2).

- Though not the focus of the encyclical, there are two sections that deal with experimentation on human embryos (63.1–2) and on the morality of prenatal diagnostic techniques (63.3–4).

- Under the pretext of compassion, "euthanasia" kills a person whose suffering we cannot   bear, or whose care is no longer considered worthwhile. But no one—not relatives, physicians nor legislators—can "arrogate to themselves the power to decide who ought to live and who ought to die" (66.3) with regard to the terminally ill, the weak, the elderly, or those who have a handicap or disease, no matter how severe.

- The same teaching holds true for suicide and "assisted suicide." "Suicide is always morally objectionable as murder. The Church's tradition has always rejected it as a   gravely evil choice" (66.1). One does not have the right, alone or with "assistance," to terminate one's own life. God is the author and Lord of life.

- Nonetheless, the encyclical states, "To forego extraordinary or disproportionate means [to extend a person's life] is not the equivalent of suicide or euthanasia" (65.2).

The goal of this encyclical is to state clearly the perennial teaching of the Catholic Church, based on the principle that human life is a gift of God, which we must cherish and protect. God's commandment, "You shall not kill," is the ultimate protection of innocent human life—and so Christians must proclaim, defend and obey this law. However, many forces in Western society are conspiring to undermine and reject the sanctity of human life.

CULTURE OF DEATH, CULTURE OF LIFE

In the final chapter of *Evangelium Vitae*, Pope John Paul reminds us of the Church's identity as "the people of life and for life...because God, in his unconditional love, has given us the Gospel of life" (78.3, 79.1). I am reminded of powerful words in the Gospel of John in which Jesus contrasts the thief "who comes only to steal and kill and destroy" with himself, the Good Shepherd who said, "I came that they may have life, and have it abundantly" (Jn. 10:10). Most of this encyclical focuses on the monumental struggle between the "culture of death," which like the thief "comes only to steal and kill and destroy," and the mission of Jesus and the Church to bring and protect life. This final section focuses on the positive mission of the Church to promote a "new culture of human life": "to preach the Gospel of life, to celebrate it in the liturgy and in our whole existence, and to serve it with the various programs and structures which support and promote life" (79.4).

THE MISSION

The mission of the Church in this regard comes down to something simple. As Pope John Paul summarizes it:

- "Jesus is the only Gospel" (80.1; cf.1 Jn. 1:1).

- "To proclaim Jesus is itself to proclaim life." Jesus is life, and by the gift of the Spirit, this life is bestowed on us; not just physical life, but "eternal life," through which "every person's earthly life acquires its full meaning" (80.2).

With "gratitude and joy," Christians are to share this good news with everyone so that it will "penetrate every part of society" (80.4). How are we to do this?

First, the Holy Father says that we must always include in our proclamation *the core* of the Gospel, that is, the announcement of a living God "who calls us to profound communion with himself and awakens in us the certain hope of eternal life." Realizing this we are able "to see in every human face the face of Christ" (81.1).

Secondly, he says we need to present the consequences of this Gospel, which are as follows:

> Human life, as a gift of God, is sacred and inviolable. For this reason procured abortion and euthanasia are absolutely unacceptable. Not only must human life not be taken, but it must be protected with loving concern. The meaning of life is found in giving and receiving love, and in this light human sexuality and procreation reach their true and full significance. Love also gives meaning to suffering and death; despite the mystery which surrounds them, they can become saving events. Respect for life requires that science and technology should always be at the service of man and his integral development. Society as a whole must respect, defend and promote the dignity of every human person, at every moment and in every condition of that person's life. (81.2)

Here we have a lucid and simple summary of the requirements and implications of the Gospel of Life. This is what the Church must proclaim from the start, supported and unfolded in catechesis, "preaching, personal dialogue and in all educational activity" (82.1). Pope John Paul insists that we need to be tireless in our proclamation and explanations regarding the sanctity and dignity of human life, recalling St. Paul's admonition to Timothy:

> Preach the word, be urgent in season and out of season, convince, rebuke, and exhort, be unfailing in patience and teaching. (82.2; 2 Tim. 4:2)

Pope John Paul II notes that this passage is particularly urgent for those who are set apart through ordination to be the "official" teachers of the truth, most of all the bishops. He wrote, "we are the first ones called to be untiring preachers of the Gospel of life" (82.2).

During the U.S. presidential campaign in 2008, some Catholic bishops in the U.S. spoke out boldly about the urgency of electing pro-life candidates and opposing those candidates who would use their influence to destroy or threaten human life. This was in the face of much opposition, even within the Catholic community. There was pressure for bishops "not to tell people how they should vote" and criticism of "single issue" voting. Pope John Paul II cuts to the heart of issue:

> In the proclamation of this Gospel [of life], we must not fear hostility or unpopularity, and we must refuse any compromise or ambiguity which might conform us to the world's way of thinking (cf. Rom. 12:2). (82.3)

Pope John Paul warns theologians, pastors, teachers and "all those responsible for catechesis and the formation of consciences…may they never be so grievously irresponsible as to betray the truth and their own mission by proposing personal ideas contrary to the Gospel of life as faithfully presented and interpreted by the Magisterium" (82.2). Now, when human life and human dignity is under such grave and brazen attack, is not the time for rationalizations that prevent the Gospel of Life from being taught and proclaimed clearly and insistently.

CELEBRATION OF LIFE

After issuing this warning, the encyclical returns to what the Church must stand for positively as a "people for life" (83.1).

First, the Holy Father reflects that to develop a true sense of "wonder" about the miracle and beauty of each individual person requires a "contemplative outlook" (83.2). From this flows "songs of joy, peace and thanksgiving for the priceless gift of life" (83.3). To promote the cause of the dignity and sanctity of life is much more, for Catholics, than a matter of political or social advocacy. It leads to worship and "to celebrate the God of life, the God who gives life" (84.1).

Pope John Paul recalls the many psalms that tell how God has foreknown and brought forth each person in the womb (cf. Ps. 139:13–16; Ps. 8:56). For Catholics, the celebration of the sacraments and the feasts of the liturgical year are celebrations of the life God has given to us as his people (84.3). The symbols and rituals of various peoples and cultures show us the variety of ways humanity celebrates the gift of life. Pope John Paul proposes that Catholics in each country celebrate its own "Day for Life" annually. "Its primary purpose should be to foster in individual consciences, in families, in the Church and in civil society a recognition of the meaning and value of human life at every stage and in every condition" (85.2).

LIVING THE GOSPEL OF LIFE

Christians celebrate the gift of life daily, in their self-giving love of others (86.1). With this transition, the encyclical turns our attention to ways of promoting life through acts of selfless service, which are often routine, hidden and unheralded. Here Pope John Paul II speaks of "brave mothers" as "heroic women" who "do not always find support in the world around them." He speaks bluntly of the attacks on motherhood "promoted and broadcast by the media...In the name of progress and modernity the values of fidelity, chastity, sacrifice, to which a host of Christian wives and mothers have borne and continue to bear outstanding witness, are presented as obsolete...We thank you, heroic mothers, for your invincible love!" (86.3).

Heroism is shown in fidelity to the values of the Gospel that are spurned and scorned by many in modern society. "Times have changed," people say, but as C.S. Lewis was fond of saying, "you can't tell truth by a clock, like telling time." The truth and values of the Gospel do not change with the passing of time.

Living the Gospel of Life means living in charity. There is a specific attitude that distinguishes our service of charity: "we must care for the other as a person for whom God has made us responsible" (87.2). And for whom has God made us responsible? *Everyone* is our neighbor (cf. Lk. 10:29–37—the parable of the Good Samaritan), and especially the one who is poorest and most in need (Mt. 25:40). Pope John Paul II insists that where human life is involved "the service of charity must be profoundly consistent…for human life is sacred and inviolable at every stage and in every situation; it is an indivisible good" (87.3). The Christian must continue to "write history" by supporting life in all situations. Specifically mentioned are programs to support mothers who choose to have and raise their children, even without the help of the father, and respect for the life of the marginalized or suffering "especially in its final phases" (87.4).

ALL ARE INVOLVED

There are many ways of involvement in building a "culture of life":

- centers for natural methods of regulating fertility (88.2)

- marriage and family counseling agencies (88.2)

- centers assisting in or providing newborn care (88.2)

- organizations devoted to treating drug addiction, mental illness, AIDS patients, and the disabled (88.3)

- providers of care for the elderly and terminally ill (88.4)

- hospitals, clinics and convalescent homes (88.5)

- the work of all health care personnel, whose "profession calls them to be guardians and servants of human life" (89.2)

- volunteer workers of various sorts (90.1)

- all forms of social activity and commitment in the political fields on behalf of life, including civil leaders (90.2, 90.3)

- the family, which has a "decisive responsibility" (92.1), as "the sanctuary of life" (92.2; cf. *CA* 39)

- the exercise of conscientious objection in relation to procured abortion and euthanasia (89.3)

The Holy Father also discusses the issue of population growth, which must "respect the primary and inalienable responsibility of married couples and families...It is therefore morally unacceptable to encourage, let alone impose, the use of methods such as contraception, sterilization, and abortion in order to regulate births" (91.1). Positively, "Governments and...international agencies must...strive to create...conditions which will enable married couples to make their choices about procreation in full freedom and with genuine responsibility" (91.1). A fairer distribution of wealth and provision of greater opportunities would help couples in this task.

A CALL TO THE CHURCH AND THE WORLD

The encyclical concludes that the "service of the Gospel of life is thus an immense and complex task" which is *everyone's* task and responsibility (91.2). "We need to begin with the renewal of a culture of life within Christian communities" (95.3). This will involve adopting and promoting a life-style that values "the primacy of being over having, of the person over things" (98.1). Christians must "walk as children of light...and try to learn what is pleasing to the Lord. Take no part in the unfruitful works of darkness" (95.1; Eph. 5:8, 10–11).

This is the reference point for Christians: what is pleasing to the Lord. John Paul II prophetically calls for "a general mobilization of consciences and a united ethical effort to activate a great campaign in support of life. All together, we must build a new culture of life" (95.2).

In what way is this culture of life *new*?

- *new*, because it will be able to confront and solve today's unprecedented problems affecting human life

- *new*, because it will be adopted with a deeper and dynamic conviction by all Christians

- *new*, because it will be capable of bringing about a serious and courageous cultural dialogue among all parties

- *new*, because it is rooted in the Church's mission of evangelization, the purpose of which is "to transform humanity from within and to make it new" (95.2; cf. *EN* 18)

Some say that the "pro-life" movement among Christians has lost its fervor and is in decline. May all Christians, along with all people of good will desiring to do what is right, be stirred and encouraged by this message of Pope John Paul II in *Evangelium Vitae*. It is a call to work tirelessly for the protection of the most fundamental human right, the right to life, so that a new "culture of life" will flourish in which every innocent person's life will be protected and valued from the moment of conception to natural death. There can be neither *true democracy* nor *true peace* unless *life is defended and promoted* (cf. 101.5–6).

Mary, the Mother of Jesus, is our example in welcoming the life of her son, and in persevering in her vocation amid suffering and trial. In the Book of Revelation, she is the "woman" (Rev. 12:1) involved in a cosmic struggle against "a great red dragon" (Rev. 12:3)—Satan.

> Mary thus helps the Church to realize that life is always at the center of a great struggle between good and evil, between light and darkness. The dragon wishes to devour "the child brought forth" (cf. Rev. 12:4), a figure of Christ, whom Mary brought forth "in the fullness of time" (Gal. 4:14)…But in a way that child is also a figure of every person, every child…because—as the Council reminds us—"by his incarnation the Son of God has united himself in some fashion with every person" (*GS* 22). (104.2)

The decision is clear: "rejection of human life, in whatever form that rejection takes, is really a rejection of Christ" (104.3). On the other hand, John Paul reminds us, "Whoever receives one such child in my name receives me" (Mt. 18:5); "Truly, I say to you, as you did it to one of the least of these my brethren, you did it to me" (Mt. 25:40). (104.3).

—————————— QUESTIONS FOR REFLECTION ——————————

1. Reflect on the inestimable value and dignity of each human person—and the extent and gravity of the attacks against life that continue to mark human history.

2. Governments that "claim the right to abortion, infanticide and euthanasia, and to recognize that right in law" (20.3) distort human freedom. How does this undermine the true purpose of government, and separate humanity from God?

3. Consider the different signs of hope Pope John Paul II enumerates, and the "inescapable responsibility of choosing to be unconditionally pro-life."

4. Regarding both legitimate defense (national defense or self-defense) and the death penalty, why is it important for our consciences to be formed by the recent teachings of the Church?

5. Consider Pope John Paul's thoughts on two means, abortion and euthanasia, of directly killing innocent human beings.

6. Reflect on ways the Church proclaims and lives the Gospel of Life. What is your/my personal responsibility in proclaiming and living the "Gospel of Life"?

FOR FURTHER READING

- Fr. Austin Fagothey, S.J., *Right and Reason*, Chapters 14 (Freedom), 19 (Rights), 20 (Life)
- Pope John Paul II, Letter to Families (*Gratissimam Sane*)
- Sacred Congregation for the Doctrine of the Faith, Gift of Life (*Donum Vitae*)
- Sacred Congregation for the Doctrine of the Faith, *Declaration on Procured Abortion*
- *Catechism*, Part III, Article 5: 2258–2330; 2366–2379
- *USCCA*, Chapter 29 (Promote the Culture of Life)

12

Ut Unum Sint
"That They May Be One ..."

The Twelfth Encyclical Letter of Pope John Paul II

May 25, 1995

If the first millennium of Christianity was marked by the substantial unity of the Church, and the second millennium was the era of Christian division, what does the third millennium hold? Will it be the time of the restoration of the unity of the Church of Jesus Christ? Is this an unrealistic expectation? No, Christians hope for unity because at the Last Supper Jesus himself prayed for all who would believe in him: "that they may all be one [*ut unum sint*]; even as you Father are in me, and I in you" (Jn. 17:21).

Before undertaking our review of Pope John Paul II's twelfth encyclical letter, *Ut Unum Sint*, it would be helpful to establish the context for this encyclical by discussing the emergence of the ecumenical movement and the teaching on ecumenism of the Second Vatican Council. One evident fruit of Jesus' prayer for unity in our time is the emergence of the ecumenical movement at the beginning of the twentieth century. The Second Vatican Council's "Decree on Ecumenism" (*Unitatis Redintegratio*) defines ecumenism as "a movement, fostered by the grace of the Holy Spirit, for the restoration of unity among all Christians" (*UR* 1). This movement gathered support when Protestant missionaries met and discussed the scandal of Christians contending for converts in mission lands, all claiming to be the "true church" or to preach the full gospel of Jesus Christ. The Catholic Church did not become involved in the Protestant and Orthodox ecumenical efforts based on the same claim that the Catholic Church is the one, true Church. In this view the only legitimate ecumenism was for the Christians who had broken from the Catholic Church to return to her. This was the position of Pope Pius XI in his 1928 encyclical letter, *Mortalium Animos.*

However, it became evident that this approach to other Christians did not succeed in promoting unity, but only further alienated them from Catholics. Pope Pius XII launched a new direction when he sent official Catholic observers to meetings of the World Council of Churches, the major ecumenical association of Protestant and Orthodox Christians at the time.

VATICAN II

This new direction was confirmed when Pope John XXIII called the Second Vatican Council and pronounced Christian unity as one of the three primary objectives of the Council, along with the renewal of the Catholic Church and promoting peace and unity among all peoples and nations. These three aims were interrelated: Christians could not credibly promote peace and unity among peoples and nations if they were at war and divided among themselves, and the Catholic Church could not effectively promote unity among Christians unless she was purified and renewed.

This renewal of the Catholic Church, the first step in ecumenism, involves a reform both of our lives and our attitudes. Regarding Catholic life, the "Decree on Ecumenism" observes:

> For although the Catholic Church has been endowed with all divinely revealed truth and with all means of grace, yet its members fail to live by and with all the fervor that they should, so that the radiance of the Church's image is less clear in the eyes of our separated brethren and of the world at large, and the growth of God's kingdom is delayed. All Catholics must therefore aim at Christian perfection. (*UR* 4)

For this reason, the Decree states, "Church renewal has…notable ecumenical importance" (no. 6). Regarding attitudes, the Council rejects a "Catholic triumphalism," which directly opposes the humility that should mark Christ's disciples. The Catholic Church is unique because Christ, her founder, has endowed her with all the means of salvation: the fullness of the elements of sanctification and truth that God intends for his people (cf. *LG* 8, 14; *UR* 3).

Nevertheless, Catholics should not boast of possessing something that is God's gift. As Vatican II's "Dogmatic Constitution on the Church" reminds us:

> All the Church's children should remember that their exalted status is to be attributed not to their own merits but to the special grace of Christ. If they fail moreover to respond to that grace in thought, word and deed, not only shall they not be saved but they will be the more severely judged. (*LG* 14.2)

To whom much is given, much is expected! Just as the Son of God humbled himself when he lived among us, Catholics should be known for their humility among their "separated brethren" (cf. *UR* 7.2). This is not merely a pretense, since Catholics recognize that "some, and even very many of the significant elements and endowments which together go to build up and give life to the Church itself, can exist outside the visible boundaries of the Catholic Church" (*UR* 3.2). "Nor should we forget that anything wrought by the grace of the Holy Spirit in the hearts of our separated brethren can be a help to our own edification. Whatever is truly Christian is never contrary to what genuinely belongs to the faith; indeed, it can always bring a deeper realization of the very mystery of Christ and the Church" (*UR* 4.9). Catholics actually can learn and be edified by the truly Christian endowments found in other Christian churches and ecclesial communities.

The Council also recognized that "men of both sides were to blame" for the original divisions in Christ's Church, and holds that we cannot charge with the "sin of separation" those Christians who subsequently have been born into these churches and ecclesial communities separated from the Catholic Church (*UR* 3.1). In fact, "the Catholic Church embraces upon them as brothers, with respect and affection" (Ibid), and the "Decree on Ecumenism" urges Catholics to make "every effort to avoid expressions, judgments and actions which do not represent the condition of our separated brethren with truth and fairness and so make mutual relations with them more difficult" (*UR* 4.2).

IS ECUMENISM A DENIAL OF REAL DIFFERENCES?

One could easily get the impression that ecumenism means avoiding divisive issues that might offend other Christians or further divide us. This is not true ecumenism, because the goal of ecumenism is to seek unity *in truth*; all involved must be totally honest about what they believe. As the "Decree on Ecumenism" explains:

> Nothing is so foreign to the spirit of ecumenism as a false ireni-cism [another translation says, "a false conciliatory approach"], in which the purity of Catholic doctrine suffers loss and its genuine and certain meaning is clouded.

> At the same time, Catholic faith must be explained more pro-foundly and precisely, in such a way and in such terms as our separated brethren can also really understand. (UR 11.1–2)

Ecumenism actually helps Catholics understand and articulate our faith more clearly, as we seek to explain its roots in Sacred Scripture, in the life and writings of the early Church, and through sound reason based on these sources. Also the Decree reminds us:

> When comparing doctrines with one another, they [Catholic theologians] should remember that in Catholic doctrine there exists a "hierarchy" of truths, since they vary in their relation to the fundamental Christian faith. (UR 11.3)

This is also a valuable principle for the catechist, who begins by teaching the most essential and fundamental truths of our faith, and then shows how other truths are related to and flow from these.

WHAT IS NEW FROM VATICAN II?

In the Vatican II's teaching on ecumenism what is new in the Catholic Church's way of understanding and approaching other Christians? In his book, *Crossing the Threshold of Hope,* Pope John Paul II observed:

> Pope John XXIII…used to say: 'what separates us as believers in Christ is much less than what unites us.' In this statement we find the heart of ecumenical thinking. The Second Vatican Council continued in the same direction. (p. 146)

First, then, Catholics understand that we have more in common with other Christians' beliefs than what divides us. We now recognize that some of the different ways that Christians express their faith are actually complementary rather than conflicting. This was illustrated, for example, in the "Joint Declaration on the Doctrine of Justification" signed by representatives of the Lutheran World Federation and the Catholic Church on October 31, 1999. It is also true of many teachings of the Catholic Church and Orthodox churches (see *UR* 11, and *Orientale Lumen*). Pope John Paul II has described the unification of the ancient Christian traditions of the West (preserved in Catholicism) and of the East (preserved in Orthodoxy and the Eastern Catholic Churches) as enabling the Church of Christ to "breathe with both lungs." So the first major change in the Catholic Church's approach to other Christians is to *begin with what we have in common*, rather than focusing on our differences.

The second major shift in ecumenism in the teaching of Vatican II was the call for the Catholic Church to take the initiative in our relations with other Christians "praying for them, keeping them informed about the Church, making the first approaches toward them" (*UR* 4.5). This was far different from earlier in the twentieth century, in which the Catholic Church seemed to stand aloof from other Christians, waiting for them to return to us. However, if the essential gift of the Catholic Church is the gift of unity—the first "mark" of the Church and "something she can never lose" (*UR* 4.3)—it is only logical that Catholics should take the initiative to promote this unity by reaching out to other Christians. This was marvelously demonstrated by Pope John XXIII who invited representatives of other Christian churches to attend Vatican II and seated them in a prominent, visible position on the Council floor. It was demonstrated by Pope Paul VI who met with the Ecumenical Patriarch Athenagoras I in 1965, when they withdrew the mutual excommunications of 1054. And it was demonstrated in the tireless efforts for Christian unity of Pope John Paul II, which he recounted in *Ut Unum Sint* (52–76). All Catholics are called to follow their teaching and example in this area.

The third major shift indicated by Vatican II is that ecumenism is *a necessary part of Catholic life*. In all that we do, our effort and concern is to promote unity among Christians. I have often heard the word "ecumenism" spoken of by Catholics in a derogatory way, even as an "evil" or "mistake" promoted by the Second Vatican Council. Such an attitude is not acceptable, is not truly Catholic. Pope John Paul II put it bluntly in *Ut Unum Sint*:

> It is absolutely clear that ecumenism, the movement promoting Christian unity, *is not just some sort of "appendix"* which is added

to the Church's traditional activity. Rather, ecumenism is an organic part of her life and work, and consequently, must pervade all that she is and does; it must be like the fruit borne by a healthy and flourishing tree which grows to its full stature (20.1).

The Pope acknowledges, as the "Decree on Ecumenism" states, that possessing this attitude requires conversion or "a change of heart" (*UUS* 15; *UR* 7):

> Each one therefore ought to be more radically converted to the Gospel and, without ever losing sight of God's plan, change his or her way of looking at things. Thanks to ecumenism, our contemplation of "the mighty works of God" (*mirabilia Dei*) has been enriched by new horizons, for which the Triune God calls us to give thanks: the knowledge that the Spirit is at work in other Christian Communities, the discovery of examples of holiness,... There is [also] an increased sense of the need for repentance: an awareness of certain exclusions which seriously harm fraternal charity, of certain refusals to forgive, of a certain pride, of an unevangelical insistence on condemning the "other side," of a disdain born of an unhealthy presumption. Thus, the entire life of Christians is marked by a concern for ecumenism; and they are called to let themselves be shaped, as it were, by that concern. (*UUS* 15.3)

THE CONTRIBUTION OF *UT UNUM SINT*

As we have just noted from the two quotations from Pope John Paul's letter *Ut Unum Sint*, this document thrusts Christian unity—ecumenism—into the forefront of Christian concern and awareness as the Great Jubilee of the year 2000 approached. The lively concern for this issue and the intense and widespread ecumenical activity that ensued immediately after the Second Vatican Council seemed to have slackened somewhat thirty years after the close of the Council. The difficulties in moving forward toward full ecclesial communion—which for Catholics is the only suitable goal of the quest for unity for which Jesus prayed (cf. *UUS* 3, 4)—appeared ever more daunting, if not insurmountable.

As he did so often in such circumstances, Pope John Paul gave a rousing message of hope and encouragement. He reaffirmed the Catholic Church's commitment to the ecumenical endeavor and called all Catholics to participate in it according to the norms of Vatican II's "Decree on Ecumenism" (see below). In addition, *Ut Unum Sint* advanced the ecumenical movement through two unique and striking emphases. The first of these is the subject of Chapter II of the document on "The Fruits of Dialogue." Here the Holy Father encouraged the ecumenical movement by examining its "fruit" and showing how much progress has been made toward Christian unity through dialogue and other efforts since the Council. We have experienced a deeper level of "brotherhood" among Christians who have participated in the dialogue (*UUS* 41). He recalls, "two particularly telling events of great ecumenical significance for relations between East and West:" the 1984 celebration by both Eastern and Western Christians of the eleventh centenary of the evangelizing work of Sts Cyril and Methodius (whom John Paul declared "co-patrons of Europe"), and the celebration in 1988 of the thousandth anniversary of Russian Christianity with the baptism of Saint Vladimir in Kiev in 988. These anniversaries commemorate the era in which the one Church of Christ was not divided into separate "Eastern" and "Western churches"—when indeed the Church "breathed with her two lungs" (*UUS* 53–54). Recalling an ancient Christian tradition, Pope John Paul II urged churches of the East and West today to look upon each other as "sister churches." He quotes Pope Paul VI who stated in 1967:

> For centuries we lived this life of "Sister Churches", and together held Ecumenical Councils which guarded the deposit of faith against all corruption. And now, after a long period of division and mutual misunderstanding, the Lord is enabling us to discover ourselves as "Sister Churches" once more, in spite of the obstacles which were once raised between us. (*UUS* 57.1; *AI* 7)

This, Pope John Paul said, must be our goal today: to re-establish this mutual recognition as "Sister Churches."

The second new and striking emphasis of Pope John Paul II in *Ut Unum Sint* is his invitation to all Christians to a renewed dialogue with him on the ministry of the Bishop of Rome—the papacy. He recalls the address to the World Council of Churches in 1984 in which he acknowledged that the Catholic Church's conviction that the ministry of the Bishop of Rome is "the visible sign and guarantor of [the Church's] unity, constitutes a difficulty for most other Christians, whose memory is marked by certain painful recollections. To the extent we are responsible for these, I join my Predecessor Paul VI in asking forgiveness" (*UUS* 88).

In spite of these painful memories, Pope John Paul pointed out that many Christians now are open to a re-examination of the question of the role and primacy of the Bishop of Rome, particularly as a ministry that could promote Christian unity. Pope John Paul devotes five articles of *Ut Unum Sint* (90–94) to reflection on the biblical and patristic basis for the Bishop of Rome's ministry of unity, referring to this office as "the first servant of unity" (94.2). Pope John Paul II therefore recognizes that he has a "particular responsibility" in the quest for Christian unity "heeding the request made of me to find a way of exercising the primacy which, while in no way renouncing what is essential to its mission, is nonetheless open to a new situation" (95.2).

Then he invites the leaders and theologians of other Churches and ecclesial communities "to engage with me in a patient and fraternal dialogue on this subject [of Papal primacy and teaching], a dialogue in which, leaving useless controversies behind, we could listen to one another, keeping before us only the will of Christ for his Church and allowing ourselves to be deeply moved by His plea 'that they may all be one...so that the world may believe that you have sent me' (Jn. 17:21)" (96).

In the following article, the Holy Father clarifies some "non-negotiable" elements from the perspective of the Catholic Church in this dialogue. One of these is "that the communion of the particular Churches with the Church of Rome, and of their Bishops with the Bishop of Rome is—in God's plan—an essential requisite of full and visible communion. Indeed full communion, of which the Eucharist is the highest sacramental manifestation, needs to be visibly expressed in a ministry in which all the Bishops recognize that they are united in Christ and all the faithful find confirmation for their faith" (97.1).

St. Peter plays this role in the New Testament among the apostles, as the Holy Father states, "This function of Peter must continue in the Church so that under her sole Head, who is Jesus Christ, she may be visibly present in the world as the communion of all his disciples. Do not many of those involved in ecumenism today feel a need for such a ministry? A ministry which presides in truth and love so that the ship—that beautiful symbol which the World Council of Churches has chosen as its emblem—will not be buffeted by storms and will one day reach its haven" (97.1–2).

An additional point that is very characteristic of Pope John Paul II is that the unity of Christians is necessary "so that the world may believe that you [the Father] have sent me" (Jn. 17:21). Pope John Paul II proclaimed a "new evangelization"—a new missionary thrust for the Church. A united Church is really necessary for this to be fully effective. "How indeed can we proclaim the Gospel of reconciliation without at the same time being committed to working for reconciliation between Christians?" the Holy Father asks (98.2).

This encyclical letter, along with its "companion" document on the Catholic Church's relationship with Eastern Christian Churches, *Orientale Lumen* (published in the same year), provides a boost and a challenge for a renewed ecumenical effort.

THE FUTURE OF ECUMENISM

The average Christian may think that he or she does not have much to contribute to the restoration of unity of the divided Christian churches and ecclesial communities. If one isn't a church leader or a theologian, what can one do? Well, besides the "change of heart" and pursuit of personal holiness discussed above, one can *pray*, alone and with others, for Christian unity.

This "spiritual ecumenism" is "the soul of the whole ecumenical movement" (*UUS* 21.1; *UR* 8). As *Ut Unum Sint* states:

> Love gives rise to the desire for unity...love *finds its most complete expression in common prayer.* When brothers and sisters who are not in perfect communion with one another come together to pray, the Second Vatican Council defines their prayer *as the soul of the whole ecumenical movement*...If Christians, despite their divisions, can grow ever more united in common prayer around Christ, they will grow in the awareness of how little divides them in comparison to what unites them...*fellowship in prayer leads people to look at the Church and Christianity in a new way.* (21–23)

Catholics also can *study* their own faith and become familiar with the outlook of our separated brethren. It is important to understand, for example, correct and false approaches to ecumenism. Can Christians of different churches receive communion together? Can they intermarry? Is conversion of individuals to Catholicism opposed to ecumenism? These and other issues are discussed in the "Decree on Ecumenism," in *Ut Unum Sint* and in the 1993 *Directory on Ecumenism*.

For many Christians, the question of the future of ecumenism still remains: Is unity possible? One sign that may give us hope and encouragement is the existence of the Eastern rites of the Catholic Church. The Second Vatican Council's "Decree on the Catholic Eastern Churches" (*Orientalium Ecclesiarum*) reveals that in the Catholic Church there exists a genuine and ancient diversity of Catholic churches in full communion with the Pope and the Latin rite of the Catholic Church, who possess a rich treasury and tradition of prayer, devotion and liturgical practice that is fully Catholic and yet differs from the Roman or Latin rite of the Catholic Church. This may be an encouragement toward Christian unity for Christians who fear that union with the Catholic Church would mean the loss or sacrifice of the authentic Christian elements and tradition, which they possess. The Catholic Eastern Churches testify that this is not the case.

Is unity possible? In his apostolic letter at the close of the Jubilee year of 2000 (*Novo Millennio Ineunte*) Pope John Paul II acknowledged that "there is still a long way to go," but encourages us to fix our gaze on Christ, and see his great high priestly prayer that we may be one (*ut unum sint*) as "at one and the same time, a binding imperative, the strength that sustains us, and a salutary rebuke for our slowness and closed-heartedness. It is on Jesus' prayer and not on our own strength that we base the hope that even within history we shall be able to reach full and visible communion with all Christians" (*NMI* 48.3). This echoes the final paragraph of the "Decree on Ecumenism" written thirty four years earlier:

> It is the urgent wish of this Holy Council that the measures undertaken by the sons of the Catholic Church should develop in conjunction with those of our separated brethren so that no obstacle be put in the ways of divine Providence and no preconceived judgments impair the future inspirations of the Holy Spirit. The Council moreover professes its awareness that human powers and capacities cannot achieve this holy objective—the reconciling of all Christians in the unity of the one and only Church of Christ. It is because of this that the Council rests all its hope on the prayer of Christ for the Church, on our Father's love for us, and

on the power of the Holy Spirit. "And hope does not disappoint, because God's love has been poured into our hearts through the Holy Spirit, who has been given to us" (Rom. 5:5). (*UR* 24.2)

QUESTIONS FOR REFLECTION

1. An authentic Catholic understanding of ecumenism is essential. Reflect on aspects of this understanding and how it developed in history.

2. How has the "fruit of dialogue" enriched the Church since the Second Vatican Council?

3. Pope John Paul invited all Christians to dialogue on the ministry of the Bishop of Rome. What are some aspects of this office and ministry?

4. What are important steps the Holy Spirit might be calling you to in the area of ecumenism (e.g. prayer, study and "change of heart")?

FOR FURTHER READING

- Paul VI, Decree on the Catholic Eastern Churches (*Orientalium Ecclesiarum*)
- Paul VI, Apostolic Brief on "Sister Churches" (*Anno Ineunte*)
- John Paul II, The Light of the East (*Orientale Lumen*)
- Second Vatican Council, Decree on Ecumenism (*Unitatis Redintegratio*)
- *Catechism*, 813–822 (The Church is One); 1633–1637 (Mixed marriages and disparity of cult); 836–338 (Who belongs to the Catholic Church?)

13

Fides et Ratio
"Faith and Reason"

The Thirteenth Encyclical Letter of Pope John Paul II

September 14, 1998

Pope John Paul II's encyclical letter, *Fides et Ratio*, opens with an unforgettable image: "Faith and reason are like two wings on which the human spirit rises to the contemplation of truth." Yet this is spoken to a "one-winged" world in which faith is increasingly seen as unreasonable and unnecessary to apprehend truth and to live a good life. Nonetheless, the Holy Father completes these first words with a clear statement of faith:

> God has placed in the human heart a desire to know the truth—
> in a word, to know himself—so that, by knowing and loving God,
> men and women may also come to the fullness of truth about
> themselves. (cf. Ex. 33:18; Ps. 27:8–9, 63:2–3; Jn. 14:8; 1 Jn. 3:2)

This premise is continued in the encyclical's introduction, entitled "Know Yourself." He observes that all the great world religions grapple with the basic human questions about good and evil, the meaning of our existence and the possibility of an "after life." The Catholic Church has a special *diakonia* or service of truth, which it undertakes especially in the proclamation of Jesus Christ as "the way, and the truth, and the life" (Jn. 14:6) (2.1). Yet, our understanding of faith will remain partial until "the final Revelation of God" at the second coming of Jesus Christ.

THE ROLE OF PHILOSOPHY

One way to come to know truth is receiving God's revelation of truth through faith; the other way is through reason. One rational approach to seeking and discovering the truth about the most important human questions is through philosophy. True philosophy springs from and generates a sense of wonder in contemplating all that is. Some philosophers have developed systems of thought, though no one philosophical "system" or approach has a complete view of reality (4.2). Pope John Paul II is most concerned about some modern philosophies that so stress the limitations of reason that many people today doubt or deny the possibility of knowing the truth about ultimate reality through reason or through faith. He calls upon the Church's bishops, to whom the encyclical is addressed, to proclaim the truth of the Gospel of Christ with such conviction and clarity that humanity's confidence in our ability to know the truth (including through philosophy) will be restored (6.2). Pope John Paul II was especially concerned that unless this is done, the younger generation "having no valid points of reference...will stumble through life to the very edge of the abyss [of meaninglessness]" (6.3).

THE REVELATION OF GOD'S WISDOM

One of the two documents of the First Vatican Council (1869–70) was *Dei Filius*, which clarified the relationship between faith and reason. *Fides et Ratio* builds upon this conciliar document, beginning with its statement that while "natural reason" can discover certain truths, "there are proposed for our belief mysteries hidden in God which, unless they are divinely revealed, cannot be known" (9). Faith and reason are not opposed, but there are some important truths revealed by God that are accessible only by faith.

> Philosophy and the sciences function within the order of natural reason; while faith, enlightened and guided by the Spirit, recognizes in the message of salvation the "fullness of grace and truth" (cf. Jn. 1:14) which God has willed to reveal in history and definitively through his Son, Jesus Christ (cf. 1 Jn. 5:9; Jn. 5:31–32). (9)

The fact that the fullness of God's revelation appeared at the specific moment of human history in Jesus Christ shows the importance of time and history in coming to know the truths revealed by God: "history becomes a path to be followed to the end, so that by the unceasing action of the Holy Spirit (cf. Jn. 16:13) the contents of revealed truth may find their full expression" (11.3). One may ask, "If the fullness of divine truth has been revealed in Jesus Christ, what more do we have to learn or to know?" or "If the Church possesses the true revelation of God, why does the Church claim to understand some things better or more clearly today than in the past?" The answer to both of those questions is that Jesus told his followers at the end of his earthly life that there were many things that he had to teach them which they could not understand at that time, but that the Holy Spirit would teach them and guide them into the fullness of truth (cf. Jn. 16:13). This happens over the whole course of the Church's life on earth. Pope John Paul II quotes Vatican II's "Dogmatic Constitution on Divine Revelation":

> "as the centuries succeed one another, the Church constantly moves forward toward the fullness of divine truth until the words of God reach their complete fulfillment in her" (11.3; *DV* 2).

We also must remember that what is revealed is the mystery of God and his plan, which human reason alone is unable to fully comprehend.

> Revelation remains charged with mystery...Faith alone makes it possible to penetrate the mystery in a way that allows us to understand it coherently. (13.1)

The truth that God reveals is a gift, as is the faith that enables a person to receive this gift of God's revelation. It is difficult for some to depart from being guided by reason alone in order to seek and accept the gift of faith. This "act of entrusting oneself to God" is "a moment of fundamental decision which engages the whole person" (13.2). It is not an irrational act, but a free act in which a person acknowledges the inability of reason to grasp truths that God has revealed. It is an acceptance of God's invitation to receive the gift of faith, indeed, to accept God himself, the mystery of God and his plan. In this acceptance, human freedom fulfills its highest purpose: "Men and women can accomplish no more important act in their lives than the act of faith; it is here that freedom reaches the certainty of truth and chooses to live in that truth" (13.2).

Not only does Christian revelation, accepted through faith, enable people to know the truth about God, but also to know the truth about themselves:

"to embrace the 'mystery' of their own life" (15.1). One of Pope John Paul II's favorite and oft-cited passages from Vatican II is from *Gaudium et Spes* (22): "the knowledge proper to faith does not destroy the mystery; it only reveals it the more…Christ the Lord…'fully reveals man to himself and makes clear his supreme calling,' which is to share in the divine mystery of the life of the Trinity" (13.5).

CREDO UT INTELLEGAM—INTELLEGO UT CREDAM

The next two chapters of *Fides et Ratio* explore the twin truths that "I believe that I may understand" and "I understand that I may believe." The first section begins with a reflection on wisdom, beginning with the Wisdom literature of the Old Testament: "Wisdom knows and understands all" (Wis. 9:11). In these writings, the wise person is one who loves and seeks the truth. These writings do not see any opposition between the "knowledge of reason" and the "knowledge of faith," but proceed on the premise that there is "a profound and indissoluble unity" between them (16.4). Faith enabled the people of Israel to understand that in their life and history "it is the God of Israel who acts" (16.4). Faith in God enabled Israel to accept the mystery of God present and at work in nature and in history. Nature itself is a type of revelation "which, when read with the proper tools of human reason, can lead to knowledge of the Creator" (19). Faith in God "enlightens" reason, enabling people to "discover the deeper meaning of all things and most especially of their own existence" (20). The sin of the first human beings in Eden was the pride of "thinking themselves sovereign and autonomous, and into thinking that they could ignore the knowledge which comes from God" (22.3). This same pride still deceives the human race into thinking that their reason can be exercised without reference to God and his wisdom, as St. Paul described in Romans 1:21–22 (22.3). St. Paul juxtaposes "'the wisdom of this world' and the wisdom of God revealed in Jesus Christ" (23.1). "The true key-point, which challenges every philosophy, is Jesus Christ's death on the Cross. It is here that every attempt to reduce the Father's saving plan to purely human logic is doomed to failure" (23.2, cf. 1 Cor.1:20). So, we must believe in order to truly understand the ultimate meaning of all things, in order to be truly wise. "The preaching of Christ Crucified and risen is the reef upon which the link between faith and philosophy can break up, but is also the reef beyond which the two can set forth upon the boundless ocean of truth" (23.3).

INTELLEGO UT CREDAM:
"I UNDERSTAND THAT I MAY BELIEVE"

Having shown the importance of faith in order to truly understand reality, the Holy Father shifts the discussion to highlight the importance and role of reason for the believer. The starting point is St. Paul's address to the Athenians (Acts 17). St. Paul observed that their statues and monuments to many "gods" and "goddesses" told him that they were very religious and sought to acknowledge and worship the true God. St. Paul recognized in the Athenians the natural longing to know God that is deeply rooted in all people (24.1)—the "restless heart" of St. Augustine. And yet St. Paul also knew that they had not yet found the true God. How do people come to know the truth about God?

"'All human beings desire to know' [Aristotle], and truth is the proper object of this desire" (25.1). No one is really satisfied with knowledge that may or may not be true; only confidence that knowledge is true brings peace, including the truth of the values that guide our lives. The fact of death makes the question of the meaning of our lives pressing and inescapable (26).

Pope John Paul describes the human being as *"the one who seeks the truth"* (28). There are different modes of truth: "truth proper to everyday life and to scientific research…philosophical truth, attained by means of the speculative powers of the human intellect…[and] religious truths" (30.1). Yet who is able to personally verify the truth of all the knowledge and information that is presented to us as "truth"? Therefore, "this means that the human being—the one who seeks the truth—is also *the one who lives by belief*" (31). "In believing, we entrust ourselves to the knowledge acquired by other people" (32.1). Coming to know the truth is, thus, a social or communal task, ideally "sustained in all its searching by trusting dialogue and sincere friendship" (33.2). The question becomes not just, "What is the truth?" but also, "Whom do I trust to tell me or show me what is true?" Pope John Paul II gives the example of the martyrs, "who are the most authentic witnesses to the truth about existence. The martyrs know that they have found the truth about life in the encounter with Jesus Christ, and nothing and no-one could ever take this certainty from them" (32. 3). The truth attained by philosophical reflection and reason and the truth revealed by the Christian faith are not opposed. In fact "the two modes of knowledge lead to truth in all its fullness" (34). Jesus Christ is the truth. In the human search for truth (particularly the truth about God and about the meaning of human existence) and in the search for a person to whom they might trust to find truth:

> Christian faith comes to meet them, offering the concrete possibility of reaching the goal which they seek. Moving beyond the stage of simply believing, Christian faith immerses human beings in the order of grace, which enables them to share in the mystery of Christ, which in turn offers them a true and coherent knowledge of the Triune God. (33.3)

In summary, human beings not only believe in order to understand truth in its full dimensions; in their quest for truth through reason, human beings also discover the importance and even the necessity of believing or trusting in some things, and in someone, in order to come to know truth. In this process, the catechist can be that "someone" who may be trusted to communicate the truth about God and human existence which every person was created to discover.

THE QUEST FOR TRUTH

Men and women are on a journey of discovery which is humanly unstoppable—a search for the truth and a search for a person to whom they might entrust themselves. Christian faith comes to meet them, offering the concrete possibility of reaching the goal which they seek. (33)

In the first three chapters of *Fides et Ratio*, Pope John Paul II has affirmed that the quest for truth, especially the truth about ultimate realities such as God, can be attained through reason (e.g. philosophy) *and* by faith in what God reveals to us, which achieves its climax in the person of Jesus Christ. These two sources of truth are not opposed, but together "lead to truth in all its fullness" (34).

Chapter IV of *Fides et Ratio* explores more fully the relationship between faith and reason as it has developed in history. Classical, pre-Christian philosophy sought to "purify" human ideas about God of "mythological elements" and "provide a rational foundation for their belief in the divinity" (36.2). This is why some of the early Church fathers appreciated and even employed some forms of classical philosophy "which offered new ways of proclaiming and understanding the God of Jesus Christ" (Ibid). However, some Christians like Tertullian rejected philosophy as "outmoded" in addressing questions about life's meaning since Christian revelation gave direct and satisfying answers to them (cf. 37–38.1). Others, like St. Justin and Clement of Alexandria, found important truths in philosophy that could be employed to explain and defend the Christian faith (cf. 38.3). Origen employed the philosophy of Plato to shape his theological arguments against Celsus and others who criticized Christianity for being "irrational" (cf. 39). Later Church fathers, including the Cappadocians and St. Augustine set to the work of "Christianizing Platonic and Neo-Platonic thought." St. Augustine produced "the first great synthesis of philosophy and theology," unsurpassed in Western thought for centuries (40). Pope John Paul summarizes the accomplishment of the early Church fathers of both East and West: "They fully welcomed reason which was open to the absolute, and they infused it with the richness drawn from Revelation" (41.2). Those authors distinguished elements in various philosophies that were consonant with revelation and those that were not.

The next stage in the history of Christian thinking regarding faith and philosophy (reason) were the "scholastic" thinkers of the Middle Ages, beginning with St. Anselm of Canterbury in the eleventh century (42.1). The "master" of describing the confluence of faith and reason is St. Thomas Aquinas, who "had the great merit of giving pride of place to the harmony which exists between faith and reason…so faith builds upon and perfects reason" (43.1–2). Further:

> Another of the great insights of St. Thomas was his perception of the role of the Holy Spirit in the process by which knowledge matures into wisdom. (44.1)

Too often we think that the goal of reason (and faith) is simply *knowledge* of divine realities. Through the Holy Spirit, we receive a knowledge of God which is connatural, which "comes from on high," as St. James puts it, and which enables us to *judge* things according to divine truth (44.1). Nonetheless, St. Thomas "sought truth wherever it might be found," in both pagan and Christian writings, profoundly convinced (as he wrote), that "whatever its source, truth is of the Holy Spirit" (44.3). Tragically this vital synthesis between faith and reason achieved at the height of the Middle Ages gradually eroded. "From the late Medieval period onwards, however, the legitimate distinction [between faith and reason]…became more and more a fateful separation" (45.1). Eventually, this led to extreme positions "which led some to focus more on faith [fideism] and others to deny its rationality altogether" (45). Faith and reason were seen to be at odds, and much modern philosophy became totally detached from Christian revelation and even opposed to it. Sometimes this purely "rationalist" philosophy has led to "nihilism" which denies all ultimate meaningfulness. Or, philosophy becomes merely a tool for analysis of particular fields or topics, instead of a means of grasping ultimate meaning or of attaining "universal wisdom and learning" (47.1).

Pope John Paul concludes this "rapid survey of the history of philosophy" with an observation and an appeal. The observation is of the "growing separation between faith and philosophical reason" (48.1). His appeal is "that faith and philosophy recover the profound unity which enables them to stand in harmony with their nature without compromising their mutual autonomy" (48.2). Faith and reason strive for truth and arrive at it in distinct ways, but they must not be separated or opposed to each other.

SHOULD THE MAGISTERIUM INTERVENE
IN PHILOSOPHICAL MATTERS?

The fifth chapter of *Fides et Ratio* addresses the Church's role in the development of philosophy. First it affirms, "The Church has no philosophy of her own nor does she canonize any one particular philosophy in preference to others" (49.1). However, "history shows that philosophy—especially modern philosophy—has taken wrong turns and fallen into error" (49.2). Because errors in philosophy directly affect our ability to know what is true, the Church must engage in a "critical discernment" and point out "elements in a philosophical system which are incompatible with her own faith" (50.2) or "which contradict Christian doctrine" (50.1). Human reason is wounded by sin, which makes this critical discernment of philosophical tenets necessary (cf. 51).

Pope John Paul II proceeds to give examples of how the popes in the nineteenth and twentieth centuries confronted such errors. Also, the First Vatican Council, in its constitution *Dei Filius*, was the first ecumenical council to address the relationship between faith and reason and between revelation and natural knowledge of God, concluding that they are distinct but inseparable, as St. Thomas Aquinas had taught (cf. 53). In the twentieth century John Paul cites examples of the three "Pius" popes and the Sacred Congregation for the Doctrine of the Faith condemning errors stemming from false philosophies (cf. 54). Pope John Paul speaks of the widespread philosophical errors he observes in his own pontificate, ranging from a "deep-seated distrust of reason" (55.1) to an excessive rationalism. He notes "signs of a resurgence of *fideism*, which fails to recognize the importance of rational knowledge and philosophical discourse for the understanding of faith," which would include a "biblicism"—a belief that truth is *only* to be found in Sacred Scripture (55.3). The rest of this chapter discusses how the Church and Christian faith *encourage* the use of reason and sound philosophy (not limited to one philosophical approach) in order to seek and come to know the truth (56, ff). He praises Pope Leo XIII's encyclical *Aeterni Patris* (1879)—"the one papal document of such authority devoted entirely to philosophy"—and "his insistence upon the incomparable value of the philosophy of St. Thomas" (57). Other fruitful philosophical approaches of more recent origin are also mentioned favorably, including John Paul's own preferred approach employing the phenomenological method (59). Also familiar is the Pope's extended discussion of the Second Vatican Council, in this case its teaching concerning philosophy. He highlights Chapter One of *Gaudium et Spes*, which

> amounts to a virtual compendium of the biblical anthropology from which philosophy too can draw inspiration. The chapter deals with the value of the human person created in the image God, explains the dignity and superiority of the human being over the rest of creation, and declares the transcendent capacity of human reason. (60.1)

We should also note Vatican II's teaching on the importance of a sound philosophical formation for priests "based upon the philosophical heritage which is enduringly valid, yet taking into account currents of modern philosophy" (*FR* 60.2; cf. "Decree on Priestly Formation" *Optatam Totius*, 15). John Paul notes that this philosophical formation will help the priests pastorally in addressing, "the aspirations of the contemporary world" and "the causes of certain behavior" (60.3). He emphasizes that "the study of philosophy is fundamental and indispensable to the structure of theological studies and to the formation of candidates for the priesthood. It is not by chance that the curriculum of theological studies is preceded by a time of special study of philosophy" (62.1). Pope John Paul concludes that, "it has seemed to me urgent to re-emphasize with this Encyclical Letter the Church's intense interest in philosophy—indeed the intimate bond which ties theological work to the philosophical search for truth. From this comes the Magisterium's duty to discern and promote philosophical thinking that is not at odds with faith" (63).

WHAT IS THE RELATIONSHIP BETWEEN PHILOSOPHY AND THEOLOGY?

What, then, is the proper relationship between philosophy (the knowledge of reason) and theology (the knowledge of faith)? Pope John Paul wishes to recall some specific "tasks" of theology that "demand recourse to philosophical enquiry" (64). First, philosophy can help us communicate the faith by providing concepts through which doctrine is understood (cf. 65). Secondly, philosophy can help people to understand more fully the salvific meaning of the truths "proposed to us in the Sacred Scriptures and rightly interpreted by the Church's teaching" (66.1). The field of "fundamental theology" has a specific duty of explaining the relationship between faith and philosophical thought. "[F]undamental theology should show how, in the light of the knowledge conferred by faith, there emerge certain truths which reason...already perceives" (67.1). Likewise, "moral theology requires a sound philosophical vision of human nature and society, as well as of the general principles of ethical decision making" (68). The proper understanding, through philosophy, of concepts and principles that can be known by reason prevents theology from being based on "faith alone"—a sort of fideism.

Pope John Paul alludes to the objection that today the theologians should "rely less on philosophy than on the help of other kinds of human knowledge, such as history and above all the sciences" (69.1). While agreeing with the positive contributions of these fields, only philosophy is concerned with the "universal" and not just the particular, and with objective truth that can place different world-views and cultures into proper perspective.

In this chapter, the Holy Father remarks on the various cultures of the world and notes that although "they offer different paths to the truth," (70.3) in the salvation brought by Jesus Christ "the walls separating the different cultures collapsed" (70.2). Jesus is savior of all, and when his gospel is proclaimed, people preserve their own cultural identity and draw from it "the elements compatible with their faith, in order to enrich Christian thought"

(72.3). In discerning these elements, Pope John Paul taught that we should keep in mind three criteria:

1. "The universality of the human spirit, whose basic needs are the same in the most disparate cultures;"

2. "the Church cannot abandon what she has gained from her inculturation into the world of Greco-Latin thought;"

3. "particular cultural tradition[s]" must retain their identity *without* being closed to what it can gain from other traditions. (72.3)

One of the most useful *images* presented in this document is that of the relationship between philosophy and theology as a *circle*. Theology's "starting point" on this circle is the word of God revealed in history. Philosophy helps us to understand God's word better, through reasoned reflection (cf.73). It is not surprising that some of the greatest Christian theologians were also great philosophers, such as St. Gregory of Nazianzus and St. Augustine in the early Church; Sts. Anselm, Bonaventure and Thomas Aquinas in the Middle Ages; and in recent times Western thinkers such as [Bl.] John Henry Newman, Antonio Rosmini, Jacques Maritain, Etienne Gilson and Edith Stein; and Eastern Christian scholars Vladimir Soloviev, Pavel Florensky, Peter Chaadaev and Vladimir Lossky (cf.74).

PHILOSOPHICAL STANCES REGARDING CHRISTIAN FAITH

Surveying the history of the relationship between faith and philosophy, Pope John Paul distinguishes "different stances of philosophy with regards to Christian faith" (75.1). The first stance occurred before the coming of Christ, when Christianity was not yet known. This reminds us that philosophy, even after Christ, remains primarily an endeavor of reason that maintains its own principles, "even when theological discourse makes use of philosophical concepts and arguments" (75.2). Philosophy remains a distinct *science*.

A second stance is what the Pope calls "*Christian philosophy*," which more properly could be called a Christian way of philosophizing. Subjectively, faith "purifies" reason, liberating people from the sin of presumption that would deny that there are some truths that reason and philosophy are incapable of knowing without faith and God's revelation. Objectively, revelation does enable us to know some truths that are beyond the capacity of reason. The Christian philosopher knows this (cf. 76).

The third stance of the relationship between faith and philosophy is "*when theology itself calls upon it* [philosophy]." Theology requires a method of presenting the revealed truths of faith, as well as needing "philosophy as a partner in dialogue in order to confirm the intelligibility and universal truth of its claims" (77.1). Philosophy in the past was called the "handmaid of theology" (*ancilla theologiae*). Without a sound philosophy, theologians "would run the risk of doing philosophy unwittingly and locking themselves within thought-structures poorly adapted to the understanding of faith" (77.3). Once again, Pope John Paul II points out the "merits of St. Thomas' thought" as "an authentic model for all who seek the truth. In his thinking, the demands of reason and the power of faith found the most elevated synthesis ever attained by human thought" (78).

CONCLUSION

The final chapter and conclusions of *Fides et Ratio* challenges philosophy to recognize its need to draw from the Word of God in Sacred Scripture in order to approach the mystery of the Word of God incarnate, Jesus Christ, who is the ultimate meaning and fulfillment of the world and of human existence. Although this chapter is mainly addressed to philosophers and theologians, Pope John Paul II does refer to the role and importance of catechesis, which is a fitting way to conclude our reflections on this important encyclical letter.

> Theological work in the Church is first of all at the service of the proclamation of the faith and of catechesis. Proclamation or kerygma is a call to conversion, announcing the truth of Christ, which reaches it summit in his Paschal Mystery: for only in Christ is it possible to know the fullness of the truth which saves (cf. Acts 4:12; 1 Tim. 2:4–6).
>
> In this respect, it is easy to see why, in addition to theology, reference to *catechesis* is also important, since catechesis has philosophical implications which must be explored more deeply in the light of faith. The teaching imparted in catechesis helps

to form the person. As a mode of linguistic communication, catechesis must present the Church's doctrine in its integrity, demonstrating its link with the life of the faithful. The result is a unique bond between teaching and living which is otherwise unattainable, since what is communicated in catechesis is not a body of conceptual truths, but the mystery of the living God. (99.1–2)

QUESTIONS FOR REFLECTION

1. Pope John Paul II begins, "Faith and reason are like two wings on which the human spirit rises to the contemplation of truth." Reflect on the importance of "contemplation of truth" and therefore the importance of a right understanding of both faith and reason.

2. Why is faith necessary, especially with regard to divine revelation?

3. What is the relationship between: "I believe that I may understand" and "I understand that I may believe"?

4. How does the Church look upon philosophy? Why is it important to her that reason and *sound* philosophy be taught and used?

5. Consider the three historically distinct stances of philosophy with regard to Christian faith.

FOR FURTHER READING

- Fr. Austin Fagothey, S.J., *Right and Reason*, Chapters 11 (Reason), 12 (Law)
- First Vatican Council, *Dei Filius*
- Pope Benedict XVI, On the Word of God in the Life and Mission of the Church (*Verbum Domini*)
- *Catechism*, Part I, Section 1 ("I Believe"—"We Believe", 26–100)
- *USCCA*, Chapter 4 (Bring About the Obedience of Faith); Chapter 5 (I Believe in God)

14

Ecclesia de Eucharistia
"The Eucharistic Church"

The Fourteenth Encyclical Letter of Pope John Paul II

April 17, 2003

"The Church draws her life from the Eucharist," which is *the heart of the mystery of the Church*" (1.1). It is to draw the Church more deeply into this mystery that Pope John Paul II issued his final encyclical letter on Holy Thursday of 2003, a day that the Holy Father traditionally issued a letter to all priests. But on the twenty-fifth anniversary of his pontificate, John Paul wished to "involve the whole Church more fully in this Eucharistic reflection, also as a way of thanking the Lord for the gift of the Eucharist and the priesthood" (7). It is fitting that we should all reflect on this great gift of the Lord to his Church.

The Eucharist, "the source and summit of the Christian life" (*LG* 11), is one way that Jesus fulfills his promise: "Lo, I am with you always to the close of the age" (Mt. 28: 20). The "holy Eucharist contains the Church's entire spiritual wealth: Christ himself, our passover and our living bread." Christ's own flesh is "now made living and life-giving by the Holy Spirit" (*EE* 1.2; *PO* 5).

THE INSTITUTION OF THE EUCHARIST

Jesus instituted the Eucharist at the Last Supper, but the apostles gathered there did not fully understand his "words of institution"—giving them his own body and blood—until after the sacred Triduum, after Christ's Resurrection. Then, like the disciples on the road to Emmaus, their eyes were opened and *they began to understand this paschal mystery* that "*stands at the center of the Church's life*" (*EE* 3).

After the Church was born at Pentecost, they "devoted themselves to the breaking of the bread [the Eucharist]" (Acts 2:42). The celebration of this mystery has continued to the present day. Like a "time-machine,"

> At every celebration of the Eucharist we are spiritually brought
> back to the paschal Triduum: to the events of the evening of Holy
> Thursday, to the Last Supper and to what followed it. (3)

This is the meaning of the Eucharist as *anamnesis—remembering in a way that makes the event present*—in the fulfillment of Jesus' words, "Do this in remembrance of me" (Lk. 22:19). We remember Jesus' blood shed, first in Gethsemane and completely on Golgotha; indeed the Eucharist brings us back spiritually to the "hour of Jesus"—the hour of his death, that is also the "hour of our redemption" (4.1).

THE EUCHARISTIC CHURCH

The Holy Father goes on to reflect that when we proclaim this mystery of our faith (*mysterium fidei*) in the redemptive power of Christ's Passion and death, the mystery of the Church is also revealed. Hence the title of the encyclical *Ecclesia de Eucharistia*—the Eucharistic Church. Yes, the Church was born at Pentecost, "yet a decisive movement in her taking shape was certainly the institution of the Eucharist" (5.2). In the Eucharist the whole Paschal Mystery—"is as it were gathered up, foreshadowed, and 'concentrated' forever" (Ibid).

THE EUCHARIST—A MYSTERY OF FAITH AND LIGHT

What is our response to this? Pope John Paul says, "The thought of this leads us to profound amazement and gratitude…This amazement should always fill the Church assembled for the celebration of the Eucharist. But in a special way it should fill the minister of the Eucharist" (5.3). By his words, spoken with the faith of the Church and with the commission of Christ through his ordination, Jesus Christ becomes truly present in visible and tangible form! John Paul II emphasizes that the *main purpose of this encyclical letter is* "to rekindle this Eucharistic 'amazement'" in the whole Church (6). Christ is truly present, and so "the faithful can in some way relive the experience of the two disciples on the road to Emmaus: 'their eyes were opened and they recognized him' (Lk. 24:31)" (6). Thus, he says, "The Eucharist is both a mystery of faith and a 'mystery of light'" (6). Is it surprising that the climax of Pope John Paul's new mysteries of the Rosary, the *Luminous Mysteries*, is the institution of the Holy Eucharist by Jesus at the Last Supper? The year of the publication of this encyclical letter was proclaimed by Pope John Paul as "The Year of the Rosary" in which the Church was called in a special way to contemplate the "Eucharistic face" of Christ with Mary (7.1).

THE UNIVERSALITY OF THE EUCHARIST

As the Holy Father closed the introduction to this letter, he paused to reflect on the many places he had celebrated the Eucharist. He comments that this has given him a strong sense of its universal, even cosmic, character:

> The Eucharist is always in some way celebrated *on the altar of the world*. It unites heaven and earth. It embraces and permeates all creation. The Son of God became man in order to restore all creation, in one supreme act of praise, to the One who made it from nothing. He, the Eternal High Priest who by the blood of his Cross entered the eternal sanctuary, thus gives back to the Creator and Father all creation redeemed. (8)

PROPER EUCHARISTIC DEVOTION

The introduction ends with an observation of how the liturgical reforms of the Second Vatican Council have been received in the Church. Overall, this "has greatly contributed to a more conscious, active and fruitful participation in the Holy Sacrifice of the Altar on the part of the faithful" (10.1). Pope John Paul notes other hopeful signs such as increase in adoration of the Blessed Sacrament in many places and Eucharistic processions on the Solemnity of the Body and Blood of Christ (*Corpus Christi*).

Unfortunately, he observes, "*there are also shadows*": the abandonment of Eucharistic adoration in some places, abuses of the Eucharist and theological errors, such as the Eucharist "stripped of its sacrificial meaning...as if it were simply a fraternal banquet" (10.3).

Some "ecumenical initiatives" have lead to "practices contrary to the discipline by which the Church expresses her faith" (10.3). Thus, another purpose of this document is "to banish the dark clouds of unacceptable doctrine and practice, so that the Eucharist will continue to shine forth in all its radiant mystery" (10.4).

THE MYSTERY OF FAITH

In the encyclical's first chapter, Pope John Paul begins his reflection on this central mystery of our faith: *Christ's presence in the Eucharist—which is not just one gift of God among many—is "the gift par excellence"* (11.2). Through the Eucharist, Christ gives us himself both in his humanity and his saving work: so much so that when we celebrate the Eucharist "the work of our redemption is carried out" (11.3; *LG* 3). Another aspect of this mystery is that the salvation of Christ that was accomplished, historically speaking, on Calvary at Jesus' death was given to the disciples at the Last Supper the night before he died. The heart of this mystery is the love that God has for humanity to die for us and give himself to us in the Eucharist. "Truly, in the Eucharist, he shows us a love which 'goes to the end' (cf. Jn. 13:1), a love which knows no measure" (11.3).

Pope John Paul clarifies that the sacrifice of Jesus on Calvary and "the sacrifice of the Eucharist are *'one single sacrifice'*" (12.2; *Catechism* 1367). In the Mass, the Eucharist, Christ is *not re-sacrificed*. Rather through them *the one Sacrifice of Jesus Christ is made present throughout all time*. This sacrifice of Christ is both a gift of God the Father to us, and also a primary way that we, the Church when we offer the sacrifice at Mass, offer ourselves to the Father in union with Christ (cf. 13). The Eucharist not only makes the Passion and death of Christ present to us, but also his Resurrection. The entire Paschal Mystery of Jesus Christ is present in the Eucharist. As St. Ambrose said, "each day he rises again for you" (14).

"REAL PRESENCE"

Vatican II's Constitution on the Sacred Liturgy (art. 7) explains that Christ is truly present at Mass not only in the Eucharist but also in the priest, the word of God proclaimed in Scripture, in other sacraments that may be celebrated at Mass, and in the people gathered in worship. If Christ is truly present in all of these ways, why do we only speak of the "real presence" (body, blood, soul and divinity) of Christ in the Eucharist? The encyclical quotes Paul VI, who explains in *Mysterium Fidei* that calling the Eucharistic presence "real" is not done "as a way of excluding all other types of presence as if they were 'not real', but because it is a presence in the fullest sense: a substantial presence whereby Christ, the God-Man, is wholly and entirely present" (15.1; *MF* 39).

With the invocation of the Holy Spirit (*epiclesis*) and the words of consecration "the whole substance of the bread" and "the whole substance of the wine" become the whole substance of the body and blood of Christ. "And the holy Catholic Church has fittingly and properly called this change transubstantiation" (15.1). This is truly a mystery of faith (*mysterium fidei*) and a mystery of love that brings us to our knees in worship, especially when we consider that we are invited to the sacred banquet to receive Christ's real presence in Holy Communion. "The saving efficacy of the sacrifice is fully realized when the Lord's body and blood are received in communion" (16). We recall Jesus' words "he who eats me will live because of me" (Jn. 6:57). As Pope John Paul comments, "This is no metaphorical food: 'My flesh is food indeed, and my blood is drink indeed' (Jn. 6:55)" (16).

In receiving Christ in the Eucharist, we also receive the Holy Spirit. It is through the Holy Spirit, implored to come in the Eucharistic *epiclesis*, that the bread and wine become the body and blood of Christ, just as "the Word became flesh" when the Holy Spirit overshadowed Mary. The Holy Spirit comes to us when we receive the Eucharist. The encyclical quotes St. Ephrem: "He who eats it with faith, eats Fire and Spirit...Take and eat this, all of you, and eat with it the Holy Spirit" (17.1). As Pope John Paul explains:

> And in the *Roman Missal* the celebrant prays: "grant that we who are nourished by his body and blood may be filled with his Holy Spirit, and become one body, one spirit in Christ". Thus by the gift of his body and blood Christ increases within us the gift of his Spirit, already poured out in Baptism and bestowed as a "seal" in the sacrament of Confirmation. (17.2)

EUCHARISTIC ESCHATOLOGY

Finally, the Eucharist anticipates the final coming of the Lord, for as St. Paul taught, we celebrate the Eucharist "until you [Lord] come in glory" (1 Cor. 11:26). This is the *eschatological* dimension of the Eucharist—a "straining towards the goal, a foretaste of the fullness of joy promised by Christ (cf. Jn. 15:11)" (18). As with the Holy Spirit, *in the Eucharist we receive a share of the life of heaven* and are already, in a veiled way, united with Mary and the saints gathered around God's throne in worship: "The Eucharist is truly a glimpse of heaven appearing on earth" (19). However, this in no way causes Catholics to lessen our sense of responsibility for the world today, but rather increases it. In a world with so little hope and where so many of the poor are oppressed, the *Eucharist is a source of hope*. "For this reason too, the Lord wished to remain with us in the Eucharist" (20.2). Perhaps this explains why the Gospel of John includes the "washing of the feet"—stressing service of the world and communion with it—in place of the words of institution of the Eucharist found in the Synoptic Gospels. Pope John Paul closes the first chapter with a powerful reflection on this "eschatological tension" of living fully in this world in service while awaiting the world to come.

> Proclaiming the death of the Lord "until he comes" (1 Cor. 11:26) entails that all who take part in the Eucharist be committed to changing their lives and making them in a certain way completely "Eucharistic". It is this fruit of a transfigured existence and a commitment to transforming the world in accordance with the Gospel which splendidly illustrates the eschatological tension inherent in the celebration of the Eucharist and in the Christian life as a whole: "Come, Lord Jesus!" (Rev. 22:20). (20.3)

THE EUCHARIST BUILDS THE CHURCH

The second chapter of *Ecclesia de Eucharistia* focuses on how the Eucharist is "at the center" of the Church's growth (21.1). When the first Eucharist was celebrated at the Last Supper, who was there with Jesus? It was the Twelve—the original apostles—who represented both the new Israel and the beginning of the Church's leadership structure (hierarchy). This is also the first instance of a sacramental communion with Christ. In many ways, the establishment of the Eucharist was the planting of a "seed" out of which the Church of Jesus emerged and grew.

Pope John Paul reflects that in the Eucharist we receive Jesus, "but also that *Christ receives each of us*" (22.1). He enters into friendship with us, or deepens that friendship. "I no longer call you servants, but friends" (Jn. 15:14). Through this union with Christ, the Church "becomes a 'sacrament' for humanity," that is, "the Church draws [from the Eucharist] the spiritual power needed to carry out her mission. The Eucharist thus appears as both *the source and the summit* of all evangelization" (22.2). It is the *summit* of evangelization since *the goal of all evangelization is communion or unity*, with God and with each other. Receiving communion together confirms and deepens the unity of the Church. This communion goes beyond natural human fellowship that we experience in sharing a meal. The presence of Christ in the Eucharist binds us together spiritually. This unifying power of Christ's body also works against the seeds of disunity sown by Satan that are so deeply rooted in fallen human nature. "The Eucharist, precisely by building up the Church, creates human community" (24.2).

The Holy Father also notes, "The *worship of the Eucharist outside of the Mass* [Eucharistic adoration] is of inestimable value for the life of the Church" (25.1). Hence, he encourages pastors, in particular, to promote the practice of Eucharistic adoration and exposition of the Blessed Sacrament both by word and example. "It is pleasant to spend time with him, to lie close to his breast like the Beloved Disciple (cf. Jn. 13:25) and to feel the infinite love present in his heart" (25.2). Pope John Paul II refers to his teaching in *Novo Millennio Ineunte* that "in our time Christians must be distinguished above all by the 'art of prayer'" (Ibid; *NMI* 32). What better place to pray than before the Lord present in the Blessed Sacrament? As St. Alphonsus Liguori taught: "Of all devotions, that of adoring Jesus in the Blessed Sacrament is the greatest after the sacraments, the one dearest to God and the one most helpful to us" (25.3).

THE APOSTOLIC ROOTS OF THE EUCHARIST

The third chapter of *Ecclesia de Eucharistia* reminds us, first, that the Eucharist would not exist without the priesthood. At the Last Supper, Jesus gave his apostles the priestly commission and authority to consecrate the Eucharist, "Do this in memory of me" (Lk. 22:19). In the Church, the Eucharist continued to be consecrated by the apostle's successors (the bishops) and those appointed and ordained by them. Even though Christ is present whenever two or three are gathered in his name (cf. Mt. 18:20), Pope John Paul points out "that the Eucharist which they celebrate is *a gift which radically transcends the power of the assembly*" and that an assembly gathered for the Eucharist "absolutely requires the presence of an ordained priest as its president" (29). Only the priest recites the Eucharistic Prayer, "while the people participate in faith and in silence" (28.2).

Discussion of the relationship between the priestly ministry and the Eucharist among Christians has resulted in "significant progress" toward Christian unity (ecumenism) on this topic (cf. 30). Catholics and Orthodox are in nearly complete agreement; and many Protestants, while rejecting "transubstantiation," highly value the Lord's Supper and believe in the presence of Christ there in some way. The document reaffirms that Catholics cannot receive the Eucharist from any minister not validly ordained, for this would slow "the progress being made toward full visible unity" (30.2). Catholics are encouraged to participate in ecumenical services of the word or of common prayer, though these may not substitute for Sunday Mass.

THE EUCHARIST SOURCE OF PASTORAL MINISTRY

The Eucharist is the *"center and summit of the priestly ministry"* (31.1; emphasis mine). Pope John Paul II quotes his 1980 letter on the Lord's Supper (*Dominicae Cenae*, 2), in which he states that the Eucharist "is the principle and central *raison d'être* of the sacrament of priesthood" (31.1). Priests run the risk today of *losing their focus*, and the key to maintaining the proper focus is the Eucharist, celebrated daily. It is the source of the "pastoral charity," which is the heart of priestly ministry, according to Vatican II. The Eucharist is also the *most effective prayer for priestly vocations*, which are so necessary because, as the Pope explains, "no Christian community can be built up unless it has its basis and center in the celebration of the most Holy Eucharist" (33). Without priests, there can be no Eucharist, and the Church community without the Eucharist is sorely lacking.

THE EUCHARIST: THE CHURCH'S SOURCE OF UNITY

Chapter IV of the encyclical focuses on the central theme of the Second Vatican Council: *communion*. The entire purpose of God's saving design is to bring humanity back into loving communion with the Trinity and with each other after the original sin disrupted and broke this communion.

The Eucharist is one of the great gifts God has provided to restore and deepen our communion with God and with each other. As the Pope observes: "It is not by chance that the term *communion* has become one of the names given to this sublime sacrament. The Eucharist thus appears as the culmination of all the sacraments in perfecting our communion with God the Father by identification with his only-begotten Son through the working of the Holy Spirit" (34.1–2). In response to this great gift, the Holy Father urges us to cultivate a constant desire for the Eucharist. He affirms St. Teresa of Avila's practice of making a "spiritual communion" if one cannot attend Mass (34.2).

Pope John Paul goes on to highlight some important points on the theology of the Eucharist. Participating in Eucharistic communion *presupposes a communion of faith and life* among those who receive. When Catholics receive the Eucharist together, we both express and deepen the unity or communion we share in the Church (cf. 35). Thus, Catholics who are cut off from communion through mortal sin must receive the Sacrament of Reconciliation (Penance) before receiving the Eucharist. The Church also has a right to refuse Holy Communion to those who "obstinately persist in manifest grave sin" (37.2; *CIC* 915). "Because the Eucharist makes present the redeeming sacrifice of the Cross…it naturally gives rise to a continuous need for conversion" (37.1).

Besides these cases of serious personal sin, the other normal requirement to share in the Eucharist is that of full, visible communion with the Catholic Church. "It is not possible to give communion to a person who is not baptized or to one who rejects the full truth of the faith regarding the Eucharistic mystery" (38.2). A person must also be in full, visible communion with his own bishop and with the pope, who preserve the unity of the Church, since "the Eucharist expresses this universal communion with Peter and with the whole Church" (39.2).

THE EUCHARIST CREATES AND FOSTERS COMMUNION

Nothing in the Church expresses and fosters unity so clearly and so effectively as sharing in the Eucharist. Pope John Paul notes that this "is one of the reasons for the importance of Sunday Mass" (41). He reflected on this topic in his Apostolic Letter on the Lord's Day (*Dies Domini*), and in *Novo Millennio Ineunte* (35). The celebration of the Eucharist is the focal point of our gathering as a Christian community every week.

But, what about *"the relationship of the Eucharist to ecumenical activity"* (43.1), that is, to the quest for Christian unity? This is the final topic to be addressed in Chapter IV, and the Holy Father states clearly the norm regarding *"intercommunion"* (Eucharistic sharing among Catholics and Christians of different churches or ecclesial communities) presented by Vatican II:

Precisely because the Church's unity…absolutely requires full communion in the bonds of the profession of faith, the sacraments and ecclesiastical governance, it is not possible to celebrate together the same Eucharistic liturgy until those bonds are fully

re-established. Any such concelebration would not be a valid
means [to unity], and might prove instead to be *an obstacle to the
attainment of full communion,* by weakening the sense of how far
we remain from this goal and by introducing or exacerbating am-
biguities with regard to one or another truth of the faith. (44.1)

In other words, Christians should not "pretend" or act as if we are fully united
by receiving the Eucharist together, when we are, in reality, still divided in
essential matters. For Catholics, receiving the Eucharist together with other
Christians is the desired goal that we seek, when all other divisions have been
overcome. It is not a means to attaining that goal or end.

Nonetheless, Pope John Paul, quoting his encyclical letter on Christian
unity, *Ut Unum Sint,* insists: "And yet we [all Christians] do have a burning desire to join in celebrating the one Eucharist of the Lord, and this desire itself is
already a common prayer of praise, a single supplication" (44.2; *UUS* 45). The
Holy Father ends this section acknowledging special circumstances in which
individual persons may be allowed to receive Holy Communion outside of
their own communion, in churches that possess a valid priesthood and therefore a true Eucharist (*EE* 45–46).

THE DIGNITY OF THE EUCHARISTIC CELEBRATION

Recognizing the greatness of the Lord's gift to us of his body and blood in
Eucharist, *"the Church has feared no 'extravagance',* devoting the best of her
resources to expressing her wonder and adoration before the *unsurpassable
gift of the Eucharist"* (48). To those who criticize the Catholic Church for her
gold-plated ciboria, monstrances and chalices, and for her beautiful church
buildings, the Pope recalls Jesus' words to Judas who complained of the
"waste" of the expensive ointment which Mary of Bethany used to anoint
Jesus' feet (47.1–2; cf. Mt. 26:8–11; Mk. 14:4–7; Jn. 12:4–8). Jesus loved the
poor, but he refused to condemn the "extravagance" of one who would honor
his body, which was to be given up to death for our salvation. Honor given to
the Eucharist is honor given to Jesus.

The Eucharist is the living person of Jesus, who continues to dwell
among us. Therefore, everything about the liturgical celebration of the Lord's
sacrifice and the "sacred banquet" in which the Lord offers to us the *panis ange-
lorum,* the bread of angels—his own Body and Blood in the Eucharist—should

be particularly special (cf. 48). The Holy Father refers to the *"rich artistic heritage"* that has developed to honor Jesus Christ in the Eucharist, including architecture, sculpture, painting and music (49.1). The Eucharist has "powerfully affected 'culture', and the arts in particular" (49.3) and has even spawned a certain holy "competition" between Christians of the West and the East. He notes that these artists, who "have shown themselves docile and open to the inspiration of the Holy Spirit" in adorning churches and producing sacred art have provided *"a genuine service to the faith"* (50.1).

This service is not merely a past occurrence, but "is also taking place *on continents where Christianity is younger*...In my numerous Pastoral Visits I have seen, throughout the world, the great vitality which the celebration of the Eucharist can have when marked by the forms, styles and sensibilities of different cultures. By adaptation to the changing conditions of time and place, the Eucharist offers sustenance...to entire peoples, and it shapes cultures inspired by Christianity" (51.1).

Christianity, and the ways of expressing our Catholic faith in art and in the liturgy itself, is not bound to a particular time and culture of the past. However, Pope John Paul ends this chapter by urging that priests and bishops carefully review liturgical practices and adaptations to insure that the "treasure" of Christ's presence in the Eucharist is given due honor. He urges, "that the liturgical norms for the celebration of the Eucharist be observed with great fidelity...Liturgy is never anyone's private property...Our time, too, calls for a renewed awareness and appreciation of liturgical norms as a reflection of, and a witness to, the one universal Church made present in every celebration of the Eucharist. Priests who faithfully celebrate Mass according to the liturgical norms, and communities which conform to those norms, quietly but eloquently demonstrate their love for the Church" (52.2).

AT THE SCHOOL OF MARY, "WOMAN OF THE EUCHARIST"

Even though Mary, the Mother of our Lord, was not present at the Last Supper, Pope John Paul II teaches that she is the surest guide to understanding the Eucharist. *"Mary is a 'woman of the Eucharist' in her whole life"* (53.3). How? The Eucharist is a profound mystery. How can this, which appears to be ordinary bread and wine, be the Body and Blood of God incarnate, given to us to eat? Mary shows us how to make an act of faith in God and his plan, even when it seems impossible. She believed when the angel told her that she would become the Mother of God (cf. 55). At Cana, when the wine ran out, she believed her son could do the "impossible." With simple faith she said: "Do whatever he tells you" (Jn. 2:5). Pope John Paul says that these words are a prophetic word to us through Mary:

> Mary seems to say to us: "Do not waver; trust in the words of my Son. If he was able to change water into wine, he can also turn bread and wine into his body and blood." (54)

Mary teaches us about the Eucharist because she is a woman of faith. Pope John Paul recalls the Scripture passage that is the key theme of his encyclical letter on Mary, *Redemptoris Mater*: "Blessed is she who believed" (Lk.1:45). Mary also was a woman of contemplation, whose example should inspire us to contemplate the Lord who comes to us each time we receive Eucharistic communion (55.3).

Mary also expresses the "sacrificial dimension" of the Eucharist, as Simeon's prophecy that "a sword will pierce your heart" was a preparation for the pain of her son's sacrifice. "In her daily preparation for Calvary, Mary experienced a kind of 'anticipated Eucharist'—one might say a 'spiritual communion'—of desire and of oblation, which would culminate in her union with her Son in his passion" (56.1).

Yet, after Jesus rose from the dead, Mary celebrated the Resurrection with the rest of the Church through the Eucharist. Pope John Paul II says that whenever the Eucharist is celebrated Mary is present "with the Church and as the Mother of the Church...If the Church and the Eucharist are inseparably united, the same ought to be said of Mary and the Eucharist" (57.2). When the Church celebrates the Eucharist it has "the spirit of Mary"—accepting in faith the gift of God's Son to us with joy and thanksgiving. In fact, Pope John Paul II recommends, "*re-reading the Magnificat* in a Eucharistic key. The Eucharist, like the Canticle of Mary, is first and foremost praise and thanksgiving" (58.1). He proceeds to explain this beautifully (which is one good reason to read the encyclical!): "The Eucharist has been given to us so that our life, like that of Mary, may become completely a *Magnificat!*" (58.2)

CONCLUSION

Pope John Paul II concludes this, his final encyclical letter, by reflecting on the centrality of the Eucharist in our lives and in the life of the Church. The

Eucharist is central because Jesus Christ is the center of our lives. This is the lasting gift of himself to us, until he comes again in glory. Pope John Paul refers to the primary goal for the Church in the new millennium that he presented in *Novo Millennio Ineunte*. The goal and "program" for the new millennium is holiness. So he says:

> Every commitment to holiness, every activity aimed at carrying out the Church's mission, every work of pastoral planning, must draw the strength it needs from the Eucharistic mystery and in turn be directed to that mystery as its culmination. In the Eucharist we have Jesus, we have his redemptive sacrifice, we have his resurrection, we have the gift of the Holy Spirit, we have adoration, obedience and love of the Father. (60.2)

> By giving the Eucharist the prominence it deserves, and by being careful not to diminish any of its dimensions or demands, we show that we are truly conscious of the greatness of this gift. (61.3)

There is no better way to conclude the summary of *Ecclesia de Eucharistia* than these words of Pope John Paul II himself:

> Let us take our place, dear brothers and sisters, *at the school of the saints*, who are the great interpreters of true Eucharistic piety. In them the theology of the Eucharist takes on all the splendor of a lived reality; it becomes "contagious"...Above all, let us *listen to Mary Most Holy*, in whom the mystery of the Eucharist appears, more than in anyone else, as a *mystery of light*. Gazing upon Mary, we come to know *the transforming power present in the Eucharist*. In her we see the world renewed in love. Contemplating her, assumed body and soul into heaven, we see opening up before us those "new heavens" and that "new earth" which will appear at the second coming of Christ. Here below, the Eucharist represents their pledge, and in a certain way, their anticipation: "Veni, Domine Iesu!" (Rev. 22:20). (62.1)

––––––––––––– QUESTIONS FOR REFLECTION –––––––––––––

1. Why is an understanding of the Eucharist as *anamnesis* important to an understanding of the sacrifice of Jesus on Calvary and the sacrifice of the Eucharist as "one single sacrifice"?

2. How can reflecting on the real presence of Christ in the Eucharist deepen "Eucharistic amazement"?

3. Pope John Paul II reflects that in the Eucharist we receive Jesus, "but also that Christ receives each of us." Reflect on this source of hope and unity, and the value of the worship of the Eucharist outside of Mass.

4. What is the indispensable place of the ordained priest for the Eucharist? How is the Eucharist the source of life for the priest?

5. "Participating in Eucharistic communion presupposes a communion of faith and life among those who receive." What prevents "open" reception of Holy Communion among Christians?

6. What are ways, past and present, that the "treasure" of Christ's presence in the Eucharist is given due honor?

7. What is the relationship of Mary and the Eucharist?

FOR FURTHER READING

- Fr. Giles Dimock, O.P., *101 Questions on the Eucharist*
- Fr. John Hampsch, *The Healing Power of the Eucharist*
- Matt Swain, *The Eucharist and the Rosary*
- John Paul II, On the Mystery and Worship of the Eucharist (*Dominicae Cenae*)
- Second Vatican Council, Constitution on the Sacred Liturgy (*Sacrosanctum Concilium*)
- *Catechism*, Part 2, Article 3: 1322–1419
- *USCCA*, Chapter 17 (The Eucharist: Source and Summit of the Christian Life)
- USCCB, Instruction on the Eucharist (*Redemptionis Sacramentum*)